AUTUMN CALABRESE PRESENTS

FIXATE™

101 PERSONAL RECIPES TO USE WITH THE 21 DAY FIX PORTION-CONTROL PROGRAM

DEDICATION

This book is dedicated to my loving, supportive family. To my dad, who taught me to go after my dreams. To my grandma (Gram), for teaching me that food and family go hand in hand. To my big brother Bobby—without his amazing culinary talents, several of these recipes would not be in here. And to my big sister Calie for being my sounding board and sharing my passion for teaching others about nutritious food.

CONTENTS

INTRODUCTION

Why would a celebrity fitness trainer write a cookbook?

When I developed the 21 Day Fix® fitness and portion-control system, my goal was to create a straightforward yet effective fitness program, *and* to give people an easy way to know—not only what to eat to stay healthy—but how much of it to eat. So in addition to the program's workouts, I created 7 color-coded containers that deliver just the right portions every time. Simple fitness and simple nutrition.

But food to me is more than just fuel, energy, and nourishment. I grew up in a big Italian family, where every meal was a gift prepared with care and love. I want you to know that, even when you're following a nutritional plan, you can still experience that feeling as you enjoy the foods you love. That's why I wrote **FIXATE**™.

Many of my family's favorite dishes are included in the 101 recipes in this book—including some of my favorite vegetarian, vegan, paleo, and gluten-free recipes, along with my everyday "go-to's"—all created to work together with my color-coded containers and portion-control system. So whether or not you're on the 21 Day Fix meal plan, you can be sure you're enjoying healthy, delicious meals, in just the right portions, to help you reach your weight-loss goals.

In my book there are four basic "ingredients" to maintaining a healthy lifestyle: you should 1) enjoy the foods you eat, 2) have a fitness routine you can commit to, 3) eat foods that are highly nutritious, and finally, 4) know how much of it to eat. Combine all the ingredients, mix well, and serve!

A PINCH OF DELISH!

FAMILY, FOOD, AND BIG MEALS WERE THE NORM IN THE CALABRESE FAMILY.

I grew up surrounded by family in my little neighborhood of Collinwood in Cleveland, Ohio. My aunt Val lived a block away, and my grandma and grandpa just two blocks down from her. Sunday dinner was always at Gram's house. My father, sister, brother, and I joined my three aunts and seven cousins every week, come rain or shine, which meant there were at least 16 of us around the table. The first question the kids asked, as soon as we walked in the door was, "What kind of macaroni are we having tonight, Gram?" (Macaroni was our universal term for pasta of any kind.) Dad owned a popular local Italian restaurant called Bobby Cal's, and he and Grandma did most of the cooking.

The kids didn't help much in the kitchen—we were usually kicked out for stealing meatballs—so we found ourselves out in the yard playing hide-and-seek or tag. Around 3 p.m., one of the adults would call us in, and all 16 of us would sit down to a family-style meal of four or five pounds of "macaroni," a huge pot of sauce, a massive bowl of meatballs, and an even bigger bowl of salad with Gram's dressing. To drink, there was an ever-present jug of wine, as well as a two-liter bottle of soda, both of which remained on the floor at Gramps'

feet—if you wanted a refill on your drink you had to ask my grandpa and wait patiently for him to pass the bottle to you. We would spend hours at that table with each other, eating and talking (okay, it wasn't talking as much as it was yelling, but in a funny and loving way that only family would understand), and then eat some more.

Although everyone was expected to help with the cooking—especially during the holidays—Gram and my dad ran...and I mean *ran* that kitchen. I was usually bouncing back and forth between playing with my cousins and popping in to the kitchen to see what my dad was making. Though I didn't know it at the time, these two master chefs (at least that's how I saw them) were laying the foundation for my culinary education. I learned the family recipes as well as the basic techniques I would later use in my cooking—how to chop the herbs, dress the salad, roll the meatballs, and season the poultry.

So today, when I aim to create delicious, nutritious meals, I owe the "delicious" part to Gram and my dad. Yes, I use nutrition as a tool, but those Sundays in Gram's kitchen taught me that life is too short not to enjoy your food!

A HEAPING SCOOP OF FITNESS

Eventually, my dad moved our family to the suburbs where he opened his second Bobby Cal's restaurant. I was no longer riding bikes, playing outside, and walking everywhere around our little neighborhood, and as a result, I wasn't burning off all those delicious Italian carbs, so pretty soon, the pounds came on!

That was when I discovered dancing, and once I started competing my relationship with food changed. I'd found something I loved and was passionate about. With the help of my dance instructor, I began to see food as playing a critical role in helping me become the best dancer that I could be.

I cut out soda because my instructor said it was bad for my muscles, and at the same time added more veggies to my diet, switched to skim milk, and became much more aware overall of the foods I was putting into my body. Combined with the fact that I was now dancing several hours a week—it's no surprise that my weight quickly dropped back to a healthy level.

At the ripe, old age of 17, I believed I had mastered the art of nutrition. But in reality, my education had just begun. I would learn—and very soon—that food alone wouldn't keep me healthy unless I combined it with regular exercise.

INGREDIENT #3:
A HANDFUL OF NUTRITION KNOW-HOW

During my first year of college, I didn't gain the "Freshman 15" because I was dancing nonstop, some days for up to eight hours. But by the time senior year rolled around, a bulging disc meant that I had to take a break from dancing, so I moved to California to pursue a career in acting. I found a job waiting tables to pay the bills, and began settling into a serious relationship. My college days of dancing day and night were behind me, so sure enough, the pounds once again began to pile on. The difference was, this time the weight refused to come off, no matter how hard I tried. It didn't make sense to me—I was eating healthy, exercising, and was on my feet waiting tables every night. What was I doing wrong?

After I got married and became pregnant with my son, it suddenly hit me—and I realized that it was only going to get harder to take that extra weight off. I knew I had to take control of the situation before the situation took control of me. I was going to have this baby, AND I was going to have my body back! I took a hard look at what I was eating, and throughout my pregnancy, I studied up on what foods were good for me, and what was good for the baby.

I (mostly) gave up dairy because, well, why are we the only mammals that continue to drink the milk of other mammals, even after we've been weaned? On those rare occasions when I do eat dairy (let's be honest, cheese does taste awesome!), I stick to organic, so I can avoid the hormones and chemicals. I switched from wheat bread to sprouted-grain bread (like Ezekiel) because sprouting makes it easier for your body to absorb the nutrients in grains. Sprouting also reduces phytic acid, an "anti-nutrient" that can prevent the body from absorbing some minerals. In addition, I gave up my processed breakfast cereal for natural, whole-food protein sources like eggs.

These changes, together with my commitment to exercise, made all the difference in the world. After my son was born, I lost all my baby weight in less than 12 weeks (and I had a C-section—just saying, no excuses). I ended up losing another five pounds to boot! And that's where my weight has stayed for the past 6 years.

A PORTION OF PORTION CONTROL (AKA "THE SALAD STORY")

At last, things were coming together for me. I was finding success as a fitness trainer, and as I did, I began to see how proper eating was every bit as important as proper exercise. I began to ask myself how I could share my newfound knowledge of nutrition with others. How could I help my clients see results by eating right? The answer came to me one day in the form of a really big restaurant salad.

I was at lunch one day with a client who was seeing good results, but not losing the weight she wanted to, even though she was eating the right kinds of foods. We ordered a couple of salads, and when they arrived, I was shocked to see how huge they were! She proceeded to eat the whole serving—while I ate only a portion. And that's when it hit me—she didn't have a problem because of *what* she was eating, it was because of *how much* she was eating. Healthy food is great, but there can always be too much of a good thing. Portions really do matter!

I pulled out my calorie count app and, sure enough, her salad clocked in at over 1,400 calories! To her mind, she was eating healthy food—lettuce and chicken and broccoli—but it was four servings' worth, and that's not counting the dressing, the crumbled goat cheese, and all the pita chips sprinkled in (the chips were little, so she didn't think she was eating too many, but she probably ended up eating a cup's worth).

Regardless of the quality of my food choices, I've always seemed to have a knack for portion control. I even managed to know when to say "when" at those amazing Sunday dinners at my grandparents' house. After years working with my clients, I realized that this isn't the case for everyone. People have become focused on quantity over quality. So I asked myself: how can I help people understand that it's not just about putting healthy foods in your body, it's about knowing how much of it to put in?

And that question led to **21 DAY FIX**.

AND FINALLY ...
MIXING IT
ALL TOGETHER

FIXATE is about combining my love of good food with the work I've done teaching people how to eat right and how to use portion control, which is why each recipe includes the Fix Container Equivalents. When converting these recipes to include the equivalents, we take a lot into consideration— including the types of ingredients (veggie, fruit, starch, etc.), as well as the levels of protein, carbs, calories, and fat. We also are extremely mindful of what feels right and intuitive to our readers. So it's not an exact science, but rather a delicate and sometimes a slightly subjective balancing act!

Food is much more to me than a series of multicolored containers, it is something to be enjoyed and celebrated. I put in enough work throughout the year so that I won't restrict myself on a holiday. I'll enjoy myself on Thanksgiving or Christmas, but I won't go crazy. I'll eat the turkey, I'll eat the stuffing, I'll eat the sweet potatoes, and I'll even eat the pumpkin pie. What I don't do is eat massive amounts of it, but I will enjoy myself— and I want you to enjoy yourself too. This cookbook seemed like the ideal way to share all the wonderful and delicious recipes of my childhood (with a few healthy adjustments), along with other recipes I've developed over the years for my friends and family.

Mixed into my recipes are many different vegan, vegetarian, and paleo options. After all, our bodies are all unique and very different, and the food choices we make will also be different. So I wanted to expose you to some different ways of eating and give you plenty of opportunities to try various dishes, so I can help you continue to eat healthily—or even better, introduce you to something new!

MY FOOD PHILOSOPHY

MASTERING THE 10%

Food means different things to different people. To me, it means staying healthy, feeling and looking my best, enjoying life, spending time with family and friends—and so much more. To be able to pull all of these things off, my philosophy is simple. Eat clean without depriving yourself from time to time. We can't always avoid chocolate, or chips, or ice cream, so it all comes down to moderation. The rest of the time, it's fresh fruits and vegetables, whole grains, meat and fish that have been raised as naturally as possible, and healthy fats. (Speaking of healthy fats, BIG fan of coconut oil here!)

When it comes to unhealthy foods, I'm all about coming up with some ground rules for moderation. For example, dessert is not something you have every day, nor is alcohol but you can indulge occasionally. But how much? How often? Simple. I go by what I call the 90/10 rule. If you're eating healthy 90% of the time, then when Friday rolls around, you can have a few bites of dessert or a glass of wine without feeling guilty or like you've derailed your weight-loss goals. Indulgence on that level just isn't going to cause a setback!

Sometimes I'll even make one of my "10%" indulgences work for me! When I'm heading into competition, I purposely try to grow my legs and my glutes, so I save my cheats for leg days. I carb-load before going to the gym, and afterwards I drive to the grocery store and get a couple donuts, so I can jam my muscles with glycogen (that's the sugar that supplies my muscles with energy) to make sure I'm fueled up for future workouts. It's strategic snacking!

Additionally, the occasional indulgence also keeps you from bingeing. If you're allowed to have a little treat here and there, you don't ever feel deprived. And that's a huge part of being able to have a healthier relationship with food. So let's break the self-abuse cycle of "Oh, my gosh, I ate this or that bad thing and now I have to pay the price and be strict with myself." Fuel your body with healthy food in the right portion sizes, so when you have a treat, really enjoy it (guiltlessly); then move on and go back to eating clean. Once you get into this groove, you'll see that it really is incredibly simple.

THERE'S MORE THAN ONE WAY TO EAT

I don't knock other diets but, for the record, I eat grains and I like meat. (I admit it!) Breads and cereals are important carb-loading tools for me. I also eat chicken. I eat steak. I eat fish. There's not a (healthy) protein out there that I am "anti" about. Okay, so maybe I draw the line at liver or anchovies, but besides that . . .

We all have different bodies, goals, and beliefs, and these happen to be my choices. But it makes perfect sense to me that there should be different ways to eat, which is why I've done my best to provide plenty of recipes here for vegans, vegetarians, and paleos—three styles of eating that I often get asked about—as well as some gluten-free options.

VEGETARIAN

Simply put, a vegetarian is someone who avoids animal products. Many vegetarians are lacto-ovo—meaning they don't eat meat or fish of any kind but they do eat eggs and dairy. If you stick to primarily fresh produce and make a point of getting enough protein, a vegetarian diet can be a great way to eat.

VEGAN

Some vegetarians avoid all animal products, even honey. These are vegans. One of the keys to this diet is to keep your protein up by eating plenty of legumes—beans, lentils, and peas—and whole grains. Both of these types of foods contain amino acids, the building blocks of protein. When you combine legumes with whole grains, you get the 9 essential amino acids humans need to survive. Soy, hemp, and quinoa contain all 9 essentials, no combining required.

PALEO

On the other hand, the paleo diet is filled with animal products. Their theory is that humans had healthier diets before farming took hold as a way of feeding our increasing population. This "Agricultural Revolution" changed our diet to include mostly grains (wheat, corn, rice, etc.) and led to more processed foods. Paleos believe our bodies weren't designed to process these things, so they avoid them while eating plenty of organic meat and fish, as well as tons of veggies.

Just like vegetarian diets, paleo diets vary in degrees of intensity. Some paleos avoid legumes for the same reasons they avoid grains. Some also swear off dairy, where others embrace a daily dose of grass-fed butter.

Where the typical vegan diet tends to be high in carbs, the typical paleo diet is quite low in carbs. In a lot of situations, this is fine. However, there are some situations, like if you're an endurance athlete, that you might really need those carbs.

When done right, these are all healthy ways to eat. I also think they work great as guidelines. You don't need to completely give up meat to benefit from a few more vegetable-based meals in your life. "Meatless Mondays" is a trend I've seen going around. On the other hand, most of us eat too many carbs and processed foods, so taking a chapter from the paleo book might be a good thing too.

DAIRY AND SOY AND GLUTEN! OH, MY!

DAIRY

I don't generally drink milk because I don't feel that we technically need it. All those good things that your mom told you were packed into a glass of milk can easily come from other sources too. For example, leafy greens are full of calcium. And, with a couple exceptions, dairy isn't that great a source of protein, given it usually contains more carbs or fat than actual protein! Also, on a personal note, when I eat too much of it, I tend to bloat—which is something you avoid when you wear a swimsuit as much as I do!

But I can tell you, I can't avoid dairy entirely. Why? Because cheese and ice cream are delicious, that's why! And from a culinary perspective, dairy is an important ingredient in a lot of recipes. So instead of going cold turkey I exercise moderation, finding ways to use a minimal amount without losing the yum factor.

SOY

Again, I don't eat a lot of it. But when I do, I stay away from all that scary, highly processed stuff. I'll stick to foods like organic tofu, edamame, tempeh, and a little soy sauce from time to time.

GLUTEN

I don't avoid gluten but, like dairy and soy, I tend not to have a lot of it in my diet. It's not that I have an allergy or intolerance, it's just that if you eat a clean, balanced diet, chances are that you're not getting much of it.

Gluten is a protein found in some grains, especially wheat. Very few people have a true gluten allergy called Celiac disease. However, some experts believe that gluten intolerances are more common than we think, and are responsible for things like chronic inflammation and even ADHD.

While I'm not sure if gluten can be blamed for all these things, I have seen enough science to know it's probably not the best thing in the world for us. And most people eat too many grains anyway—which means too many carbs, so if eliminating gluten can help you control your grain intake, I'm all for it.

NUTRITIONAL ICONS

To make it easier for you to spot vegetarian, vegan, paleo, and even gluten-free recipes, I've included icons at the top of each recipe. If you are following a gluten-free diet, remember to check all labels to confirm your ingredients are 100% gluten-free, since foods are often processed at facilities that also process wheat and other grains.

 VEGAN

 VEGETARIAN

 PALEO-FRIENDLY

 GLUTEN-FREE

KITCHEN TIPS

FIVE TIME, SPACE, AND MONEY-SAVING TIPS

When it comes to cooking, who wouldn't love an amazing workspace filled with every conceivable gadget, and spices from across the globe? The reality is that many of us don't have the budget or the space for it, so we need to be supersmart and efficient about how we outfit our kitchen!

Properly stocking your kitchen is a subject that practically requires its own book. Between my years working at my dad's restaurant, to juggling a busy career, I've learned how important "efficiency" is to a single mom. Here are a few ways to make establishing a proper kitchen a little easier, saving you time, space, and money.

1) YOUR POT AND PANS

Over time, you'll end up with all kinds of cookware, but when you're starting out, you really only need three things.

- A small saucepan
- A large saucepan (or soup pot)
- A skillet

You'll be able to do every recipe in this book equipped with these three tools. You'll be able to do everything from boiling pasta, to making elaborate stews and omelets, to sautéing chicken.

There are plenty of types of cookware out there. I personally recommend cast iron. It's heavy, but it heats evenly, it's easy to clean, and it's practically indestructible.

2) YOUR COUNTERTOP

Those big, expensive countertop machines can do everything, but do you really need one? In my honest opinion, no. Most food can be chopped, shredded, or mixed by hand or with smaller, cheaper, more storable tools. I've gotten by for years with a food processor, a hand mixer, and my blender. Between those three—and my hands—I can get any job done.

If you have the countertop real estate and budget for an expensive piece of equipment, go for it, but don't be scared away from making amazing meals just because you don't have one.

3) YOUR SPICE RACK

Learning how to blend herbs and spices is important to becoming a good cook, but that doesn't mean you need to use 20 different ingredients every time you make a bowl of oatmeal. My breakfast oats get a splash of vanilla extract and a dash of pumpkin pie spice and they're good to go.

There's no shame in the occasional shortcut in your spice collection, whether it's store-bought pumpkin pie spice, apple pie spice, or Herbes de Provence. Chefs have spent hundreds of years combining just the right flavors for all kinds of needs. Take advantage of that to make your life easier!

4) YOUR FREEZER

Same rules apply. Individual bags of frozen strawberries, frozen blueberries, and frozen blackberries have their uses, but if I'm making a tropical fruit smoothie or a berry smoothie, it's so much easier to have a "fruit medley" bag on hand instead of opening, pouring, and sealing three different bags.

And if your fruit tastes are too picky for the store-bought kind, get yourself a freezer bag and create your own. (I almost always like to have a little pineapple in my fruit medleys.)

5) YOUR FRIDGE

I can't stand wasting food, which is why I find cooking from recipes frustrating sometimes. The soup might call for one tablespoon of chopped, fresh chives, but nobody sells chives by the tablespoon! If I don't use it elsewhere, I end up with ¾ of a bunch of chives wilting in my refrigerator until I have no choice but to throw them out or compost them.

That's why I try to follow a policy I call "no vegetable left behind." Every time I'm searching through the fridge to see what I've got for a meal, I make a point of opening the produce drawers and looking for stuff that'll go bad if I don't eat it quickly. I find that most veggies (and fruit for that matter) will fit nicely chopped up and tossed into some kind of mixed food.

Fresh produce you might try in your next green salad:

- Baby spinach
- Raw zucchini
- Bell peppers (any color)
- Raw cauliflower
- Kale

Fresh produce you might try in your next stir-fry:

- Asparagus
- Mushrooms (any variety)
- Onions
- Broccoli
- Eggplant

BUON APPETITO!

Don't be afraid to experiment. Cooking is all about experimentation—trying new combinations and different variations. If the dish doesn't turn out the way you had hoped, oh well! But the upside is if you get it right, you now have a delicious new recipe to add to your collection!

To help you do this, I've peppered the recipe section of this book with tons of hints, tips, and substitutions. Over the years, I've found so many ways to make food healthier—yet still tasty—and I'm thrilled that I get to take those years of learning and share them with you.

THE CONTAINER SYSTEM

You don't need to be doing a Beachbody® program to enjoy the recipes in the **FIXATE** cookbook. Anyone can enjoy these delicious and healthy dishes. But if your goal is weight loss, athletic performance, general wellness, or all three then you'll really want to use these recipes with one of the Fix plans that include the container system, such as 21 DAY FIX, 21 DAY FIX EXTREME®, and PORTION FIX™.

How does the container system work? Easy—nutrition plays a huge role in helping you achieve your fitness and weight-loss goals. It's not just a matter of figuring out what to eat; it's also a question of figuring out how much to eat. The Fix eating plans are straightforward systems that help you accomplish both of these things using a nutritious food plan and seven color-coded containers to get your portions right.

HOW TO GET YOUR FIX

Incorporating **FIXATE** into your Container System and Eating Plan is easy. Every recipe includes colored squares at the top of the page that correspond to the container of the same color, indicating the CONTAINER EQUIVALENTS per serving.

So for every serving you eat, simply tick off the corresponding containers from your CALORIE CHART.

For example, if you have *Banana Oat Pancakes* (page 95) for breakfast, tick off 1 ⬤ yellow box and ½ ⬤ purple on your tally sheet.

When used with the Beachbody Portion-Control 7-Piece Container Kit, this cookbook will truly help you achieve your weight-loss goals in the healthiest and most delicious way possible. But so that everyone can enjoy these recipes, each one includes standardized cooking measurements and comprehensive nutrition facts, in addition to the Fix color-coded container equivalents.

To learn more about using FIXATE with the Beachbody Portion-Control 7-Piece Container Kit, contact your Team Beachbody® Coach or go to TryPortionFix.com.

THESE SQUARES CORRESPOND WITH THE COLORED CONTAINER BELOW.

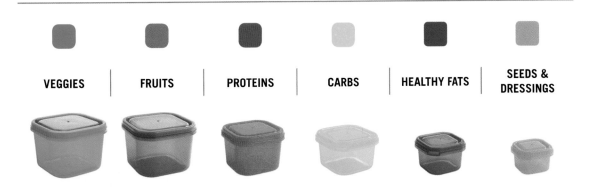

| VEGGIES | FRUITS | PROTEINS | CARBS | HEALTHY FATS | SEEDS & DRESSINGS |

SOUPS

BUTTERNUT SQUASH SOUP WITH PEPPER JAM AND SPICY YOGURT

SERVES: 9 (approx. 1 cup each)   Prep Time: 10 min.   Cooking Time: 48 min.

CONTAINER EQUIVALENTS (per serving): 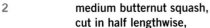 2   ● — 1

2	medium butternut squash, cut in half lengthwise, seeds removed
1 Tbsp.	olive oil
	Sea salt (or Himalayan salt) and ground black pepper (to taste; optional)
4 cloves	garlic
4	fresh thyme sprigs
4 cups	low-sodium organic vegetable broth, *divided use*
	Hot water
9 Tbsp.	Pepper Jam (recipe, pg. 89)
18 tsp.	Spicy Yogurt (recipe, pg. 89)
¼ cup	chopped fresh cilantro

1. Preheat oven to 425° F.
2. Lay squash skin side down on a baking sheet. Drizzle with oil.
3. Season with salt and pepper (if desired).
4. Place one garlic clove and one thyme sprig into the seed pocket of each squash half. Cover with aluminum foil.
5. Bake for 35 to 40 minutes, or until squash is soft, but not dried out. Remove from oven. Let squash rest until it is cool enough to handle.
6. Peel squash; discard skin and thyme.
7. Place squash, *1 cup* broth, and garlic in blender, in two or more batches, if necessary; cover with lid and kitchen towel. Blend until smooth.
8. Place squash mixture and *remaining 3 cups* broth in large saucepan; cook, over medium-high heat, stirring frequently, for 5 to 8 minutes, or until hot. If soup is too thick add water.
9. Evenly divide soup into nine serving bowls. Top each with 1 Tbsp. Pepper Jam, 2 tsp. Spicy Yogurt, and cilantro.

NUTRITIONAL INFORMATION (per serving): Calories: 104
Total Fat: 2 g   Saturated Fat: 0 g   Cholesterol: 1 mg   Sodium: 197 mg   Carbohydrates: 20 g   Fiber: 3 g   Sugars: 6 g   Protein: 4 g

Recipes containing the (GF) icon are designed to be gluten-free, but please read product labels for each ingredient to ensure this to be the case.

CREAMY TOMATO BASIL SOUP

SERVES: 8 (1 cup each)   Prep Time: 15 min.   Cooking Time: 25 min.

CONTAINER EQUIVALENTS (per serving): 1   ●—— 1½

4 tsp.	**olive oil**
½ cup	**chopped carrots**
½ cup	**chopped onions**
2 tsp.	**dried basil leaves**
1 (28-oz.) can	**whole San Marzano tomatoes**
3 cups	**low-sodium organic vegetable broth**
¾ tsp.	**sea salt (or Himalayan salt)**
1½ cups	**unsweetened almond milk**
8 tsp.	**shredded Parmesan cheese**
8 Tbsp.	**sliced fresh basil leaves**

1. Heat oil in medium saucepan over medium-high heat.

2. Add carrots, onions, and dried basil; cook, stirring frequently, for 4 to 5 minutes, or until onions are translucent.

3. Add tomatoes, broth, and salt; cook, stirring frequently, for 2 to 3 minutes, or until it reaches a gentle boil. Reduce heat to low. Gently boil for 15 minutes.

4. Place soup in blender, in two or more batches, if necessary; cover with lid and kitchen towel. Blend until smooth.

5. Return soup to saucepan. Add almond milk; cook over medium-low heat, stirring frequently, for 1 to 2 minutes, or until heated through. Do not let soup come to a boil.

6. Evenly divide soup into eight serving bowls. Top each serving with 1 tsp. cheese and 1 Tbsp. fresh basil.

NUTRITIONAL INFORMATION (per serving): Calories: 72
Total Fat: 3 g   Saturated Fat: 1 g   Cholesterol: 2 mg   Sodium: 356 mg   Carbohydrates: 8 g   Fiber: 3 g   Sugars: 5 g   Protein: 2 g

Recipes containing the **GF** icon are designed to be gluten-free, but please read product labels for each ingredient to ensure this to be the case.

EASY CHICKEN NOODLE SOUP

SERVES: 4 (1½ cups each)   Prep Time: 15 min.   Cooking Time: 20 min.

CONTAINER EQUIVALENTS (per serving): ⬛ 1   ⬜ 1½   ⬛ 1   ⬤—½

2 tsp.	olive oil
½ cup	chopped onion
2 cups	sliced celery (about 4 medium stalks)
4 cups	low-sodium organic chicken broth
3 cups	chopped rotisserie chicken breast, boneless, skinless
1½ cups	sliced carrots (about 3 medium)
1 tsp.	dried oregano leaves
½ tsp.	sea salt (or Himalayan salt)
½ tsp.	ground black pepper
1¼ cups	dry whole wheat pasta (like penne, rotini, shells, or farfalle)
¼ cup	chopped fresh cilantro

1. Heat oil in large saucepan over medium heat.

2. Add onion and celery; cook, stirring frequently, for 5 minutes, or until onion is translucent.

3. Add broth, chicken, carrots, oregano, salt, and pepper. Bring to a boil. Add pasta, reduce heat to low; gently boil for 10 minutes.

4. Evenly divide soup into four serving bowls. Add cilantro before serving.

TIP:

Substitute rice pasta or quinoa pasta for whole wheat pasta for a gluten-free choice.

NUTRITIONAL INFORMATION (per serving): Calories: 357
Total Fat: 8 g   Saturated Fat: 2 g   Cholesterol: 96 mg   Sodium: 518 mg   Carbohydrates: 26 g   Fiber: 5 g   Sugars: 5 g   Protein: 44 g

FRENCH ONION SOUP

SERVES: 4 (approx. 1½ cups each)   Prep Time: 15 min.   Cooking Time: 1 hr. 5 min.

CONTAINER EQUIVALENTS (per serving): ■ 2   □ 1   ■ ½   ▬ ½

1 Tbsp.	**olive oil**
4	**medium onions, sliced**
4 cloves	**garlic, finely chopped**
1 (8-oz.)	**smoked turkey leg (optional)**
2	**bay leaves**
2	**fresh thyme sprigs**
1 dash	**sea salt (or Himalayan salt)**
¼ tsp.	**ground white pepper**
⅓ cup	**red wine**
6 cups	**low-sodium organic beef broth**
4 slices	**low-sodium sprouted whole-grain bread**
4 Tbsp.	**shredded Gruyere (or Parmesan) cheese**

1. Heat oil in large saucepan over medium-high heat.
2. Add onions; cook, stirring frequently, for 8 to 10 minutes, or until translucent.
3. Add garlic; cook for 1 minute, or until tender.
4. Add turkey leg (if desired), bay leaves, thyme, salt, and pepper. Reduce heat to medium-low; cook, stirring occasionally, for 25 to 30 minutes, or until onions are a soft brown color.
5. Add wine. Bring to a boil over medium-high heat. Reduce heat; gently boil for 2 to 4 minutes, or until almost all liquid is absorbed. Remove turkey leg, bay leaves, and thyme.
6. Add broth. Bring to a boil over medium-high heat. Reduce heat; gently boil for 13 to 15 minutes.
7. Preheat oven to broil.
8. Place bread on a baking sheet; top with cheese. Broil for 3 to 4 minutes, or until cheese is bubbly and brown.
9. Evenly ladle soup into four serving bowls; top with bread.

RECIPE NOTE:

Usually, beef broth is counted as a red container, but not in this recipe! There's a minimal amount in this recipe and it has way less protein than other reds.

NUTRITIONAL INFORMATION (per serving): Calories: 237
Total Fat: 6 g   Saturated Fat: 2 g   Cholesterol: 16 mg   Sodium: 315 mg   Carbohydrates: 29 g   Fiber: 5 g   Sugars: 6 g   Protein: 14 g

ITALIAN WEDDING SOUP

SERVES: 6 (2 cups each)   Prep Time: 15 min.   Cooking Time: 20 min.

CONTAINER EQUIVALENTS (per serving): ■ ½ ■ 1 ●—1

1 tsp.	**olive oil**
1	**medium onion, finely chopped**
2 cloves	**garlic, finely chopped**
6 cups	**low-sodium organic chicken broth**
1 bunch	**greens (like escarole, spinach, or Swiss chard), trimmed, torn into bite-sized pieces (about 6 lightly packed cups)**
20	**Italian Meatballs (recipe, pg. 153)**
2	**large eggs**
2 Tbsp.	**grated Parmesan cheese**
½ tsp.	**sea salt (or Himalayan salt)**
½ tsp.	**ground black pepper**
1	**fresh lemon, cut into wedges**

1. Heat oil in large saucepan over medium heat.
2. Add onion; cook, stirring frequently, for 4 to 6 minutes, or until onion is translucent.
3. Add garlic; cook, stirring frequently, for 1 minute.
4. Add broth. Bring to a boil.
5. Add greens. Reduce heat to low; gently boil, covered, for 10 minutes.
6. Add meatballs; cook, stirring occasionally, for 5 minutes.
7. Combine eggs and cheese in a small bowl; mix with a fork to blend.
8. Slowly pour egg mixture into the hot soup, stirring constantly. Gently boil, covered, until egg bits are just set, about 30 seconds.
9. Season with salt and pepper; evenly divide soup into six serving bowls; serve immediately with lemon wedges.

RECIPE NOTE:

It might be tempting to fill your bowl with meatballs and call that a serving, but if you want to do it right, stick with one cup of broth and veggies, plus three meatballs.

NUTRITIONAL INFORMATION (per serving): Calories: 215
Total Fat: 11 g   Saturated Fat: 3 g   Cholesterol: 134 mg   Sodium: 493 mg   Carbohydrates: 9 g   Fiber: 2 g   Sugars: 2 g   Protein: 22 g

MEXICAN CHICKEN TORTILLA SOUP

SERVES: 4 (approx. 1½ cups each)   Prep Time: 15 min.   Cooking Time: 31 min.

CONTAINER EQUIVALENTS (per serving): ■ 2 □ 1 ■ 1½ ■ 1

8	**6-inch corn tortillas,** *divided use*
2 tsp.	**olive oil**
½ cup	**chopped onion**
2 cups	**sliced celery (about 4 medium stalks)**
2 cloves	**garlic, chopped**
4	**medium tomatoes, chopped**
6 cups	**low-sodium organic chicken broth,** *divided use*
3 cups	**chopped rotisserie chicken breast, boneless, skinless**
1½ cups	**sliced carrots (about 3 medium)**
1 tsp.	**dried Mexican oregano leaves**
1 tsp.	**ground ancho chili powder (or ground chili powder)**
½ tsp.	**sea salt (or Himalayan salt)**
½ tsp.	**ground black pepper**
½	**medium avocado, chopped**
¼ cup	**chopped fresh cilantro**
4 tsp.	**crumbled Cotija (or feta) cheese**

1. Preheat oven to 350° F.
2. Line large baking sheet with parchment paper.
3. Place tortillas on baking sheet. Bake for 8 to 10 minutes, or until toasted and crispy. Remove from oven. When cool, break into pieces. Set aside.
4. Heat oil in large saucepan over medium heat.
5. Add onion and celery; cook, stirring frequently, for 5 minutes, or until onion is translucent.
6. Add garlic; cook, stirring frequently, for 1 minute.
7. Add tomatoes; cook, stirring frequently, for 5 minutes, or until tomatoes are soft. Set aside.
8. Add onion mixture, *2 cups* broth, and *half of* toasted corn tortilla pieces to blender (or food processor); cover with lid and kitchen towel. Blend until smooth.
9. Add blended mixture to large saucepan. Add *remaining 4 cups* broth, chicken, carrots, oregano, chili powder, salt, and pepper. Bring to a boil over medium-high heat. Reduce heat to medium low; cook, stirring occasionally, for 10 minutes, or until carrots are tender.
10. Evenly divide soup into four serving bowls. Top each serving evenly with avocado, cilantro, cheese, and *remaining* toasted tortilla pieces.

TIP:

For a vegetarian version replace chicken broth with low-sodium organic vegetable broth and omit chicken breast.

NUTRITIONAL INFORMATION (per serving): Calories: 480
Total Fat: 15 g   Saturated Fat: 3 g   Cholesterol: 99 mg   Sodium: 625 mg   Carbohydrates: 42 g   Fiber: 9 g   Sugars: 8 g   Protein: 48 g

Recipes containing the **GF** icon are designed to be gluten-free, but please read product labels for each ingredient to ensure this to be the case.

MINESTRONE SOUP

SERVES: 8 (about 1 cup each) Prep Time: 15 min. Cooking Time: 23 min.

CONTAINER EQUIVALENTS (per serving): 1 1 1

2 tsp.	**olive oil**
½	**medium onion, finely chopped**
2	**medium carrots, chopped**
2	**celery stalks, chopped**
1 clove	**garlic, finely chopped**
4	**cups low-sodium organic vegetable broth**
1 (28-oz.) can	**whole tomatoes, crushed**
1 lb.	**Swiss chard, stems trimmed, leaves chopped**
1	**medium russet potato, peeled, chopped**
1 (15-oz.) can	**cannellini beans, drained, rinsed**
½ tsp.	**sea salt (or Himalayan salt)**
½ tsp.	**ground black pepper**
8 tsp.	**grated Parmesan cheese**
8 tsp.	**chopped fresh flat leaf (Italian) parsley**

1. Heat oil in large saucepan over medium heat.

2. Add onion, carrots, and celery; cook, stirring frequently, for 8 minutes, or until onion is translucent.

3. Add garlic; cook, stirring frequently, for 1 minute.

4. Add broth, tomatoes, chard, and potato. Bring to a boil, stirring occasionally. Reduce heat to low; gently boil for 10 to 12 minutes, or until chard is wilted and potato is tender.

5. Add beans; cook, stirring occasionally, for 2 minutes. Season with salt and pepper.

6. Evenly divide soup into eight serving bowls. Serve immediately sprinkled evenly with cheese and parsley.

NUTRITIONAL INFORMATION (per serving): Calories: 137
Total Fat: 2 g Saturated Fat: 1 g Cholesterol: 2 mg Sodium: 478 mg Carbohydrates: 24 g Fiber: 6 g Sugars: 7 g Protein: 6 g

Recipes containing the GF icon are designed to be gluten-free, but please read product labels for each ingredient to ensure this to be the case.

SALADS

CAESAR SALAD

SERVES: 1   Prep Time: 15 min.   Cooking Time: None
CONTAINER EQUIVALENTS (per serving): ■ 2   ■ 1   ■ 1   ■ ½   ■ 1

2 cups	**chopped romaine lettuce**
¾ cup	**shredded rotisserie chicken breast, boneless, skinless**
2 Tbsp.	**shredded Parmesan cheese**
1 tsp.	**drained capers**
1 slice	**whole-grain sprouted bread, cut into cubes, toasted**
2 Tbsp.	**Caesar Salad Dressing (recipe, pg. 79)**

1. Place lettuce on a plate; top with chicken, cheese, capers, and toasted bread.

2. Drizzle with Caesar Salad Dressing; toss gently to blend. Serve immediately.

NUTRITIONAL INFORMATION (per serving): Calories: 428
Total Fat: 17 g   Saturated Fat: 5 g   Cholesterol: 112 mg   Sodium: 480 mg   Carbohydrates: 20 g   Fiber: 5 g   Sugars: 2 g   Protein: 48 g

CALABRESE SALAD

SERVES: 1 Prep Time: 15 min. Cooking Time: None

CONTAINER EQUIVALENTS (per serving): ◼ ½ ◼ 1 ●— 1

This salad is my go-to when I'm looking for something healthy that still reminds me of growing up.
The smell and taste of the fresh mozzarella, olive oil, and basil bring me right back to my grandma's house,
but it's much healthier than sitting down to a pizza or a big plate of spaghetti and meatballs.

2 tsp.	**prepared pesto sauce,** *divided use*
2 thick slices	**large tomato,** *divided use*
4	**large fresh basil leaves,** *divided use*
1 slice	**fresh mozzarella (1 oz.)**
1 dash	**sea salt (or Himalayan salt)**
1 dash	**ground black pepper**
4 tsp.	**balsamic vinegar**

1. Spread *1 tsp.* pesto sauce on serving plate in circular motion. Top with *1* tomato slice, *2* basil leaves, and mozzarella.

2. Spread *remaining 1 tsp.* pesto sauce on mozzarella slice; top with *remaining* tomato slice and *remaining* basil leaves. Season with salt and pepper.

3. Drizzle with balsamic vinegar; serve immediately.

NUTRITIONAL INFORMATION (per serving): Calories: 138
Total Fat: 8 g Saturated Fat: 3 g Cholesterol: 18 mg Sodium: 588 mg Carbohydrates: 7 g Fiber: 1 g Sugars: 5 g Protein: 8 g

Recipes containing the GF icon are designed to be gluten-free, but please read product labels for each ingredient to ensure this to be the case.

CREAMY CHICKEN SALAD

GF

SERVES: 4 (3¼ cups each)   Prep Time: 15 min.   Cooking Time: None

CONTAINER EQUIVALENTS (per serving): ▊ 2 ▊ ½ ▊ 1 ▊ ½ ▊ ½

3 cups	**chopped rotisserie chicken breast, boneless, skinless**
½ cup	**chopped green apple**
½ cup	**seedless red grapes, cut in half**
⅓ cup	**sliced raw almonds**
2	**green onions, sliced**
2 Tbsp.	**chopped fresh tarragon**
¼ cup	**Honey Mustard Salad Dressing (recipe, pg. 87)**
8 cups	**shredded romaine lettuce**

1. Combine chicken, apple, grapes, almonds, green onions, tarragon, and Honey Mustard Salad Dressing in a large bowl; mix well. Refrigerate, covered, for 2 hours.

2. Serve 1¼ cups Creamy Chicken Salad over 2 cups romaine lettuce for each serving.

TIP:

Creamy Chicken Salad can be used to make Creamy Chicken Salad Wraps (recipe, pg. 127).

RECIPE NOTE:

Almost any leafy greens will work great with this recipe, so don't limit yourself to romaine. You can replace some or all of your lettuce with spinach, kale, or even shredded cabbage to dial up the nutrition in your salad bowl.

NUTRITIONAL INFORMATION (per serving): Calories: 312

Total Fat: 12 g   Saturated Fat: 2 g   Cholesterol: 91 mg   Sodium: 176 mg   Carbohydrates: 16 g   Fiber: 4 g   Sugars: 10 g   Protein: 37 g

Recipes containing the GF icon are designed to be gluten-free, but please read product labels for each ingredient to ensure this to be the case.

55

EDAMAME SALAD

SERVES: 4 Prep Time: 20 min. Cooking Time: None

CONTAINER EQUIVALENTS (per serving): ⬛ 1½ ⬜ 2 ⬛ 1 ⬜ 1

4 cups	**shelled edamame**
2 cups	**sliced Napa cabbage**
2 cups	**shredded (or thinly sliced) carrots**
2 cups	**thinly sliced red bell pepper**
1	**medium avocado, chopped**
1 cup	**chopped fresh cilantro**
¼ cup	**black sesame seeds**
4 Tbsp.	**Asian Vinaigrette (recipe, pg. 75)**

1. Evenly divide edamame, cabbage, carrots, and bell pepper between four serving plates.

2. Top evenly with avocado, cilantro, and sesame seeds.

3. Drizzle each salad with 1 Tbsp. Asian Vinaigrette.

NUTRITIONAL INFORMATION (per serving): Calories: 416
Total Fat: 20 g Saturated Fat: 3 g Cholesterol: 0 mg Sodium: 238 mg Carbohydrates: 42 g Fiber: 27 g Sugars: 11 g Protein: 22 g

Recipes containing the GF icon are designed to be gluten-free, but please read product labels for each ingredient to ensure this to be the case.

HEALTHIFIED COBB SALAD

SERVES: 1   Prep Time: 15 min.   Cooking Time: None

CONTAINER EQUIVALENTS (per serving):   ■ 2   ■ ½   ■ ½   ■ 1

1 cup	**chopped romaine lettuce**
1 cup	**raw baby spinach**
1	**hard-boiled egg, cut into quarters**
1 slice	**cooked lean turkey bacon, chopped**
1 Tbsp.	**chopped avocado**
1 Tbsp.	**crumbled blue cheese**
2 Tbsp.	**Lemon Dijon Salad Dressing (recipe, pg. 75)**

1. Place lettuce and spinach on a serving plate; top with egg, bacon, avocado, and cheese.

2. Drizzle with Lemon Dijon Salad Dressing; serve immediately.

NUTRITIONAL INFORMATION (per serving): Calories: 256
Total Fat: 21 g   Saturated Fat: 5 g   Cholesterol: 234 mg   Sodium: 444 mg   Carbohydrates: 6 g   Fiber: 2 g   Sugars: 2 g   Protein: 12 g

Recipes containing the (GF) icon are designed to be gluten-free, but please read product labels for each ingredient to ensure this to be the case.

59

ON-THE-GO SALAD

SERVES: 1   Prep Time: 15 min.   Cooking Time: None

CONTAINER EQUIVALENTS (per serving): ■ 3 ■ 1 ■ ½ ■ ½

1 cup	**fresh baby spinach**
1 cup	**fresh arugula**
½ cup	**snap peas (or sugar snap peas)**
½ cup	**shredded carrots**
2	**skewers from Pineapple Chicken Skewers (recipe, pg. 159) (bamboo skewers removed)**
1 tsp.	**sesame seeds**
4 tsp.	**Asian Vinaigrette (recipe, pg. 75)**

1. Combine spinach, arugula, snap peas, and carrots in a serving bowl; toss gently to blend.
2. Top with Pineapple Chicken.
3. Sprinkle with sesame seeds; drizzle with Asian Vinaigrette.

TIP:

Leftover chicken from Pineapple Chicken Skewers will be delicious in this salad. You could also use rotisserie chicken breast.

NUTRITIONAL INFORMATION (per serving): Calories: 326
Total Fat: 12 g   Saturated Fat: 2 g   Cholesterol: 73 mg   Sodium: 944 mg   Carbohydrates: 25 g   Fiber: 6 g   Sugars: 15 g   Protein: 29 g

QUINOA AND BLACK BEAN SALAD

SERVES: 12 (1 cup each)   Prep Time: 30 min.   Cooking Time: 12 min.

CONTAINER EQUIVALENTS (per serving): ▮ ½   ▯ 2   ⬤—1½

I usually make a bunch of quinoa at the beginning of the week, so I'm always looking for things to mix it into instead of just eating it by itself. I usually throw some quinoa in with fruit or veggies or whatever I have handy. Out of all the combinations, this recipe is my hands-down favorite.

⅓ cup	**fresh lime juice**
1 Tbsp.	**ground cumin**
1 Tbsp.	**sea salt (or Himalayan salt)**
⅓ cup	**olive oil**
2 cans (15-oz. ea.)	**black beans, drained, rinsed**
4½ tsp.	**red wine vinegar**
	Ground black pepper (to taste; optional)
4 cups	**water**
2 cups	**dry quinoa, rinsed**
1	**medium red bell pepper, finely chopped**
1	**medium orange bell pepper, finely chopped**
1	**medium yellow bell pepper, finely chopped**
1 (10-oz.) bag	**frozen corn, thawed**
1 bunch	**fresh cilantro, finely chopped**

1. To make dressing, combine lime juice, cumin, and salt in a medium bowl; whisk to blend.

2. Slowly add oil, while whisking constantly. Set aside.

3. Combine beans, vinegar, and pepper (if desired) in a medium bowl; mix well. Set aside.

4. Bring water to a boil in medium saucepan over high heat.

5. Add quinoa. Reduce heat to medium-low; cook, covered, for 10 to 12 minutes, or until all water has been absorbed. Remove from heat. Cool for 15 to 30 minutes. Set aside.

6. Place cooled quinoa in a large bowl. Fluff with a fork.

7. Add bell peppers, corn, cilantro, bean mixture, and dressing; toss gently to blend.

TIP:

This salad is delicious when eaten immediately. It holds well, refrigerated, and can be eaten for 2 to 3 days.

NUTRITIONAL INFORMATION (per serving): Calories: 261
Total Fat: 8 g   Saturated Fat: 1 g   Cholesterol: 0 mg   Sodium: 578 mg   Carbohydrates: 38 g   Fiber: 8 g   Sugars: 2 g   Protein: 10 g

Recipes containing the (GF) icon are designed to be gluten-free, but please read product labels for each ingredient to ensure this to be the case.

RED FRUIT SALAD

SERVES: 4   Prep Time: 15 min.   Cooking Time: None

CONTAINER EQUIVALENTS (per serving): ■ 2   ■ 1   ■ ½   ■ ½

6 cups	**fresh baby arugula**
2 cups	**finely chopped jicama**
2 cups	**sliced strawberries**
1½ cups	**fresh raspberries**
½ cup	**cubed watermelon**
1 Tbsp.	**crumbled goat cheese**
10	**raw pecan halves, chopped**
4 Tbsp.	**Raspberry Vinaigrette (recipe, pg. 77)**

1. Evenly divide arugula, jicama, strawberries, raspberries, and watermelon between four serving plates.
2. Top evenly with cheese and pecans.
3. Drizzle each salad with 1 Tbsp. Raspberry Vinaigrette.

VARIATION:

You could substitute crumbled feta or blue cheese for the goat cheese.

NUTRITIONAL INFORMATION (per serving): Calories: 179
Total Fat: 10 g   Saturated Fat: 2 g   Cholesterol: 3 mg   Sodium: 52 mg   Carbohydrates: 22 g   Fiber: 9 g   Sugars: 11 g   Protein: 4 g

Recipes containing the GF icon are designed to be gluten-free, but please read product labels for each ingredient to ensure this to be the case.

STEAK SALAD

SERVES: 4   Prep Time: 15 min.   Cooking Time: None

CONTAINER EQUIVALENTS (per serving): 2 ▮ 1 ▮ 1 ▮ 1

8 cups	**mixed salad greens**
1 cup	**sliced yellow (or red) bell pepper**
1 cup	**cherry tomatoes, cut in half**
1 cup	**sliced (or shredded) carrots**
1 cup	**sliced red onion**
3 cups	**sliced cooked steak from Steak Fajitas (steak only) (recipe, pg. 165)**
1	**medium avocado, sliced**
8 Tbsp.	**Raspberry Vinaigrette (recipe, pg. 77)**

1. Evenly divide salad greens, bell pepper, tomatoes, carrots, and onion between four serving plates.
2. Top evenly with steak and avocado.
3. Drizzle each salad with 2 Tbsp. Raspberry Vinaigrette.

TIP:

If you don't use the leftover steak (from the Steak Fajitas recipe), you could also use a very lean cooked beef sirloin.

NUTRITIONAL INFORMATION (per serving): Calories: 403
Total Fat: 23 g   Saturated Fat: 5 g   Cholesterol: 68 mg   Sodium: 134 mg   Carbohydrates: 19 g   Fiber: 7 g   Sugars: 8 g   Protein: 33 g

Recipes containing the **GF** icon are designed to be gluten-free, but please read product labels for each ingredient to ensure this to be the case.

TOASTED KALE SALAD WITH LEMON DIJON SALAD DRESSING

SERVES: 2 Prep Time: 15 min. Cooking Time: 25 min.

CONTAINER EQUIVALENTS (per serving): ■ 2 ■ ½ ■ ½ ■ ½ ●— ½

1 slice	low-sodium sprouted whole-grain bread, cut into 1-inch cubes
1 tsp.	olive oil
1 pinch	sea salt (or Himalayan salt)
1 pinch	ground black pepper
1 (4-oz.)	raw chicken breast, boneless, skinless, cut into strips
¼ tsp.	ground chili powder
1 bunch	kale, torn into large pieces (about 6-oz.)
2 Tbsp.	Lemon Dijon Salad Dressing (recipe, pg. 75)
1 tsp.	finely chopped lemon peel (for garnish; optional)

1. Preheat oven to 450° F.

2. Line a baking sheet with aluminum foil.

3. Combine bread, oil, salt, and pepper in a medium bowl; toss until well blended. Place on prepared baking sheet. Bake for 10 to 12 minutes, or until croutons are toasted and crunchy.

4. Sprinkle chicken with chili powder. Set aside.

5. Heat large nonstick skillet over medium-high heat.

6. Add chicken; cook, stirring frequently, for 6 to 8 minutes, or until chicken is no longer pink in the middle, and is blackened on the outside. Remove chicken from pan. Keep warm.

7. Add kale to skillet; cook, over high heat, for 4 to 5 minutes, turning once, or until kale is crispy and lightly charred.

8. Evenly divide kale between two serving plates; top with chicken and croutons.

9. Drizzle evenly with Lemon Dijon Salad Dressing. Evenly top with lemon peel (if desired).

TIP:

You can make this salad vegetarian by eliminating the chicken.

NUTRITIONAL INFORMATION (per serving): Calories: 210
Total Fat: 10 g Saturated Fat: 2 g Cholesterol: 49 mg Sodium: 375 mg Carbohydrates: 17 g Fiber: 3 g Sugars: 0 g Protein: 16 g

TUNA SALAD

SERVES: 2 Prep Time: 15 min. Cooking Time: None

CONTAINER EQUIVALENTS (per serving): ■ ½ ■ 1 ●— ½

2 cans (5-oz. ea.)	**chunk light tuna, packed in water, drained**
1 tsp.	**extra-virgin olive oil**
1 Tbsp.	**Dijon mustard, gluten-free**
1	**medium red bell pepper, finely chopped**
2 Tbsp.	**chopped fresh tarragon**

1. Combine tuna, oil, mustard, bell pepper, and tarragon in a medium bowl; mix well.

SERVING SUGGESTIONS
For one serving of Tuna Salad:

- Cut the top off of a medium tomato. Remove seeds. Serve Tuna Salad inside.
  CONTAINER EQUIVALENTS (per serving): ■ 1 ■ 1 ●— ½

- Serve Tuna Salad inside 2 large romaine lettuce leaves.
  CONTAINER EQUIVALENTS (per serving): ■ 1 ■ 1 ●— ½

- Cut a medium cucumber in half lengthwise. Remove seeds. Serve Tuna Salad inside.
  CONTAINER EQUIVALENTS (per serving): ■ 2 ■ 1 ●— ½

NUTRITIONAL INFORMATION for Tuna salad only (per serving): Calories: 174
Total Fat: 3 g   Saturated Fat: 1 g   Cholesterol: 32 mg   Sodium: 237 mg   Carbohydrates: 6 g   Fiber: 1 g   Sugars: 2 g   Protein: 28 g

SAUCES, CONDIMENTS, DRESSINGS

ASIAN VINAIGRETTE

SERVES: 8 (approx. 2 Tbsp. each)   Prep Time: 10 min.   Cooking Time: None

CONTAINER EQUIVALENTS (per serving): ■ 1

⅓ cup	**rice vinegar**
⅓ cup	**reduced-sodium tamari soy sauce, gluten-free**
1 tsp.	**raw honey (or pure maple syrup)**
2 tsp.	**freshly grated ginger**
5 Tbsp.	**toasted sesame oil**

1. Combine vinegar, soy sauce, honey, and ginger in a medium bowl; whisk to blend.
2. Slowly add oil while whisking; mix well.
3. Store in the refrigerator, tightly covered, until ready for use.

TIP:

Store leftover dressing in a covered container in the refrigerator. If dressing thickens when cold, hold at room temperature for 30 minutes and stir before serving. This dressing is wonderful on salads, but also is great drizzled over sautéed veggies, steamed fish, or grilled chicken or beef.

NUTRITIONAL INFORMATION (per serving): Calories: 90
Total Fat: 9 g   Saturated Fat: 1 g   Cholesterol: 0 mg   Sodium: 353 mg   Carbohydrates: 3 g   Fiber: 0 g   Sugars: 2 g   Protein: 1 g

LEMON DIJON SALAD DRESSING

SERVES: 6 (approx. 2 Tbsp. each)   Prep Time: 10 min.   Cooking Time: None

CONTAINER EQUIVALENTS (per serving): ■ 1

1	**large egg yolk, pasteurized**
1 Tbsp.	**Dijon mustard, gluten-free**
¼ tsp.	**sea salt (or Himalayan salt)**
½ tsp.	**ground black pepper**
4 Tbsp.	**fresh lemon juice**
1½ tsp.	**finely chopped lemon peel**
¼ cup	**extra-virgin olive oil**

1. Place egg yolk, mustard, salt, pepper, lemon juice, and lemon peel in a blender (or food processor); cover. Blend until smooth.
2. Slowly add oil, blending continuously until well blended.

NUTRITIONAL INFORMATION (per serving): Calories: 94
Total Fat: 10 g   Saturated Fat: 2 g   Cholesterol: 31 mg   Sodium: 157 mg   Carbohydrates: 1 g   Fiber: 0 g   Sugars: 0 g   Protein: 1 g

Recipes containing the icon are designed to be gluten-free, but please read product labels for each ingredient to ensure this to be the case.

BLUEBERRY JAM

SERVES: 16 (1 Tbsp. each)   Prep Time: 5 min.   Cooking Time: 15 min.

CONTAINER EQUIVALENTS (per serving): 1 Serving = Free   6 Tbsp. = ▪ ½

1 cup	**frozen blueberries**

1. Place blueberries in small saucepan; cook, over medium heat, stirring occasionally, for 12 to 15 minutes, or until berries have broken down and liquid becomes thicker.
2. Refrigerate, covered, to cool.

TIP:

This is a great technique that works with all kinds of fresh fruits to make delicious, healthy toppings. Try it with raspberries, plums, or apples. Cook times vary, but just make sure to keep stirring until fruit is soft and jammy and add more water if the pan gets too dry.

NUTRITIONAL INFORMATION (per serving): Calories: 5
Total Fat: 0 g Saturated Fat: 0 g Cholesterol: 0 mg Sodium: 0 mg Carbohydrates: 1 g Fiber: 0 g Sugars: 1 g Protein: 0 g

RASPBERRY VINAIGRETTE

SERVES: 11 (approx. 2 Tbsp. each)   Prep Time: 10 min.   Cooking Time: None

CONTAINER EQUIVALENTS (per serving): ▪ 1

½ cup	**fresh raspberries**
2 Tbsp.	**raw honey**
1 Tbsp.	**reduced fat (2%) plain Greek yogurt**
3 Tbsp.	**fresh lemon juice**
1½ tsp.	**finely grated lemon peel**
1 Tbsp.	**chopped fresh tarragon (or 1 tsp. dried tarragon)**
½ tsp.	**ground black pepper**
	Sea salt (or Himalayan salt) (to taste; optional)
½ cup	**extra-virgin olive oil**

1. Place raspberries, honey, yogurt, lemon juice, lemon peel, tarragon, pepper, and salt (if desired) in blender (or food processor); cover. Blend until smooth.
2. Slowly add oil, blending constantly until well mixed.

TIP:

Store leftover dressing in a covered container in the refrigerator. If dressing thickens when cold, hold at room temperature for 30 minutes and stir before serving.

NUTRITIONAL INFORMATION (per serving): Calories: 104
Total Fat: 10 g Saturated Fat: 1 g Cholesterol: 0 mg Sodium: 27 mg Carbohydrates: 4 g Fiber: 0 g Sugars: 3 g Protein: 0 g

Recipes containing the GF icon are designed to be gluten-free, but please read product labels for each ingredient to ensure this to be the case.

CAESAR SALAD DRESSING

SERVES: 10 (2 Tbsp. each)   Prep Time: 10 min.   Cooking Time: None

CONTAINER EQUIVALENTS (per serving): ▢ 1

½ cup	**reduced fat (2%) plain Greek yogurt**
3 Tbsp.	**fresh lemon juice**
⅓ cup	**shredded Parmesan cheese**
2 cloves	**garlic, coarsely chopped**
2	**anchovies**
⅓ cup	**extra-virgin olive oil**
½ tsp.	**ground black pepper**
1 dash	**sea salt (or Himalayan salt) (optional)**

1. Place yogurt, lemon juice, cheese, garlic, anchovies, oil, pepper, and salt (if desired) in a blender (or food processor); cover. Blend until smooth.

NUTRITIONAL INFORMATION (per serving): Calories: 91
Total Fat: 8 g   Saturated Fat: 2 g   Cholesterol: 4 mg   Sodium: 113 mg   Carbohydrates: 1 g   Fiber: 0 g   Sugars: 1 g   Protein: 3 g

Recipes containing the **GF** icon are designed to be gluten-free, but please read product labels for each ingredient to ensure this to be the case.

GRANDMA'S TOMATO SAUCE

SERVES: 12 (approx. ½ cup each)   Prep Time: 40 min.   Cooking Time: 1 hr. 15 min. (minimum)

CONTAINER EQUIVALENTS (per serving): 3   ½

When I was growing up, we had this sauce at every single holiday—and every Sunday. It's how my grandma's house smelled and it's how my dad's restaurant smelled. To be honest, it's not the healthiest sauce in the world but boy does it taste good! So my older brother Bobby helped me tweak the recipe a little bit. It still tastes great, but without the not-so-healthy secret ingredients that were in the original.

2 Tbsp.	**olive oil**
1	**medium onion, chopped**
4 cloves	**garlic, finely chopped**
1 (6-oz.) can	**tomato paste, no salt added**
¼ cup	**red wine**
2 cans (28-oz. ea.)	**whole peeled tomatoes (like San Marzano or Cento), crushed or pureed in blender (or food processor)**
2 Tbsp.	**agave nectar**
1 tsp.	**sea salt (or Himalayan salt)**
¼ tsp.	**ground black pepper**
1 (3-oz.)	**Parmesan (or parmigiano) cheese rind**
3 Tbsp.	**finely chopped fresh basil**

1. Heat oil in large saucepan over medium-high heat.
2. Add onion; cook, stirring frequently, for 5 to 6 minutes, or until onion is translucent.
3. Add garlic and tomato paste; cook, stirring constantly, for 2 to 3 minutes. Do not let tomato paste burn.
4. Add wine; cook, stirring constantly, for 2 to 3 minutes.
5. Add tomatoes, agave, salt, and pepper. Bring to a boil, stirring frequently. Reduce heat to low; gently boil, stirring occasionally, for 3 minutes.
6. Add cheese rind; cook, stirring occasionally, for 1 hour.
7. Add basil; mix well.

TIPS:

- Choosing the right canned tomatoes can be tricky. Look out for tomatoes that appear pale and watery, or taste bland and overly acidic. Also, I always buy whole peeled tomatoes and blend or crush them myself because producers save the best tomatoes for whole canning.
- The parmigiano rind is not totally necessary, but it is a great way to add depth to the sauce without much by way of extra calories.
- If cooking the sauce for a long time, to further develop the flavors, add 1 to 2 cups water, ¼ cup at a time, to achieve desired consistency; cook, on very low heat, covered, stirring about every 5 to 10 minutes, for 4 to 6 hours.

RECIPE NOTE:

Grandma's Tomato Sauce is considered a green container because it's free of additives and preservatives, and you can recognize every single ingredient because most of them are fresh or minimally processed.

NUTRITIONAL INFORMATION (per serving): Calories: 123

Total Fat: 4 g   Saturated Fat: 1 g   Cholesterol: 5 mg   Sodium: 343 mg   Carbohydrates: 13 g   Fiber: 3 g   Sugars: 11 g   Protein: 4 g

Recipes containing the **GF** icon are designed to be gluten-free, but please read product labels for each ingredient to ensure this to be the case.

HEALTHIER HOLLANDAISE SAUCE

SERVES: 5 (2 Tbsp. each)   Prep Time: 15 min.   Cooking Time: 15 min.

CONTAINER EQUIVALENTS (per serving): ▢ 1

	Hot water
¼ cup	reduced fat (2%) plain Greek yogurt
2 Tbsp.	fresh lemon juice
1	large egg yolk
	Sea salt (or Himalayan salt) and ground white pepper (to taste; optional)
3 Tbsp.	organic grass-fed butter, melted

1. Fill a large saucepan ¼ full of water. Bring to a boil over medium-high heat. Reduce heat; gently boil.
2. Place a heat-resistant bowl over the saucepan so that it rests snuggly like a lid.
3. Combine yogurt, lemon juice, and egg yolk in a medium bowl; whisk to blend. Season with salt and pepper (if desired).
4. Add yogurt mixture to bowl over saucepan; cook, stirring constantly, for 5 to 6 minutes, or until sauce thickens.
5. Once sauce begins to thicken, remove bowl from the saucepan, stirring for 30 seconds. Return to top of the saucepan and stir for 30 seconds. Repeat these steps for 4 to 5 minutes, or until sauce reaches the consistency of mayonnaise.
6. Remove from heat; add butter, stirring constantly, for 3 to 4 minutes, or until sauce has cooled.

TIP:

Hollandaise is an extremely versatile sauce that goes well with chicken, vegetables, and fish. It can be kept in the fridge for up to 3 days and when you are ready to use it again, it can be reheated with the double-boiler method or by simply whisking in a Tbsp. of simmering water. Just don't reheat it in a microwave or over direct flame, because that might curdle the yolk, breaking the sauce.

NUTRITIONAL INFORMATION (per serving): Calories: 87
Total Fat: 8 g   Saturated Fat: 5 g   Cholesterol: 55 mg   Sodium: 86 mg   Carbohydrates: 1 g   Fiber: 0 g   Sugars: 1 g   Protein: 2 g

HOMEMADE SALSA

SERVES: 8 (approx. ½ cup each)   Prep Time: 20 min.   Cooking Time: None

CONTAINER EQUIVALENTS (per serving): ½

1	medium jalapeño, roasted, seeds and veins removed, finely chopped
3	medium tomatoes, finely chopped
½ tsp.	sea salt (or Himalayan salt)
3 cloves	garlic, finely chopped
1	small sweet onion, finely chopped
1 bunch	fresh cilantro, stems removed, finely chopped

1. Combine jalapeño, tomatoes, and salt in a medium bowl; mix well.
2. Add garlic, onion, and cilantro; mix well.

TIP:

Another way to make the salsa is to coarsely chop the jalapeño, 2 tomatoes, and garlic. Place these ingredients and salt in food processor (or blender); cover. Pulse until well blended. Combine this mixture with the remaining tomato, onion, and cilantro; mix well.

VARIATION:

Combine 1 roasted jalapeño (seeds and veins removed, finely chopped), 2 mangoes (peeled, finely chopped), ½ medium red onion (finely chopped), 4 Tbsp. fresh lime juice, and 1 bunch cilantro (stems removed, finely chopped) in a medium bowl; mix well.

NUTRITIONAL INFORMATION (per serving): Calories: 14
Total Fat: 0 g   Saturated Fat: 0 g   Cholesterol: 0 mg   Sodium: 146 mg   Carbohydrates: 3 g   Fiber: 1 g   Sugars: 2 g   Protein: 1 g

Recipes containing the GF icon are designed to be gluten-free, but please read product labels for each ingredient to ensure this to be the case.

HONEY MUSTARD SALAD DRESSING

SERVES: 8 (2 Tbsp. each)   Prep Time: 10 min.   Cooking Time: None

CONTAINER EQUIVALENTS (per serving): 1

½ cup	reduced fat (2%) plain Greek yogurt
3 Tbsp.	Dijon mustard, gluten-free
3 Tbsp.	raw honey
3 Tbsp.	rice vinegar
¼ cup	extra-virgin olive oil
	Sea salt (or Himalayan salt) (to taste; optional)

1. Combine yogurt, mustard, honey, and vinegar in a medium bowl; mix well.

2. Slowly add oil, whisking constantly until well blended; season with salt (if desired).

NUTRITIONAL INFORMATION (per serving): Calories: 102
Total Fat: 7 g Saturated Fat: 1 g Cholesterol: 1 mg Sodium: 175 mg Carbohydrates: 9 g Fiber: 0 g Sugars: 7 g Protein: 1 g

---

LEMON GARLIC SAUCE

SERVES: 5 (2 Tbsp. each)   Prep Time: 10 min.   Cooking Time: None

CONTAINER EQUIVALENTS (per serving): 1

2 Tbsp.	fresh lemon juice
1	large egg yolk, pasteurized
2 cloves	garlic, crushed
1 Tbsp.	Dijon mustard, gluten-free
1 Tbsp.	whole-grain mustard, gluten-free
	Sea salt (or Himalayan salt) and ground pepper (to taste; optional)
3 Tbsp.	extra-virgin olive oil

1. Combine lemon juice, egg yolk, garlic, and mustards in a small bowl; mix well.

2. Season with salt and pepper (if desired).

3. Slowly add oil, whisking continuously until well blended.

NUTRITIONAL INFORMATION (per serving): Calories: 92
Total Fat: 9 g Saturated Fat: 1 g Cholesterol: 37 mg Sodium: 203 mg Carbohydrates: 2 g Fiber: 0 g Sugars: 0 g Protein: 1 g

Recipes containing the **GF** icon are designed to be gluten-free, but please read product labels for each ingredient to ensure this to be the case.

PEPPER JAM

SERVES: 18 (approx. 1 Tbsp. each)   Prep Time: 15 min.   Cooking Time: None

CONTAINER EQUIVALENTS (per serving): ½

1	medium red bell pepper, roasted over gas burner until skin is black
3	chipotle chile peppers in adobo sauce, coarsely chopped
1-inch slice	fresh ginger, peeled, cut into pieces
½	medium carrot, coarsely chopped
1 tsp.	olive oil
1 tsp.	finely chopped lemon peel
4	medium dried figs, cut in half, insides removed, skin discarded
1 pinch	sea salt (or Himalayan salt)

1. Place blackened bell pepper in resealable plastic bag; close bag. Let sit for 10 minutes to cool.

2. Run bell pepper under water to remove all skin. Cut in half. Remove and discard stem and seeds. Coarsely chop bell pepper.

3. Place bell pepper, chipotle chile peppers, ginger, carrot, oil, lemon peel, figs, and salt in food processor (or blender); cover. Blend until smooth.

NUTRITIONAL INFORMATION (per serving): Calories: 14
Total Fat: 0 g Saturated Fat: 0 g Cholesterol: 0 mg Sodium: 81 mg Carbohydrates: 3 g Fiber: 1 g Sugars: 2 g Protein: 0 g

---

SPICY YOGURT

SERVES: 9 (approx. 2 tsp. each)   Prep Time: 10 min.   Cooking Time: 3 min.

CONTAINER EQUIVALENTS (per serving): ½

½ tsp.	fennel seeds
½ tsp.	cumin seeds
½ cup	reduced fat (2%) plain Greek yogurt
1 pinch	sea salt (or Himalayan salt)
1 pinch	ground black pepper

1. Heat small nonstick skillet over medium-high heat.

2. Add fennel and cumin; cook, stirring frequently, for 2 to 3 minutes, or until fragrant. Remove from skillet.

3. Grind toasted seeds in blender (or with a small food processor, or mortar and pestle).

4. Combine yogurt, toasted seeds, salt, and pepper in a small bowl; mix well. Refrigerate, covered, for at least 30 minutes.

NUTRITIONAL INFORMATION (per serving): Calories: 10
Total Fat: 0 g Saturated Fat: 0 g Cholesterol: 1 mg Sodium: 20 mg Carbohydrates: 1 g Fiber: 0 g Sugars: 1 g Protein: 1 g

Recipes containing the **GF** icon are designed to be gluten-free, but please read product labels for each ingredient to ensure this to be the case.

PUMPKIN SEED SAUCE

SERVES: 7 (2 Tbsp. each)   Prep Time: 15 min.   Cooking Time: 5 min.

CONTAINER EQUIVALENTS (per serving): ▢ 1

¾ cup	**raw pumpkin seeds (pepitas)**
¼ tsp.	**hot pepper sauce (like Sriracha)**
½ cup	**water**
2 Tbsp.	**lime juice**
1 tsp.	**finely chopped lime peel**
1 tsp.	**extra-virgin olive oil**
¼ cup	**chopped fresh cilantro**
3 cloves	**garlic, coarsely chopped**
¼ cup	**chopped onion (⅓ medium onion)**
½ tsp.	**sea salt (or Himalayan salt)**
½ tsp.	**ground black pepper**
¼ tsp.	**ground cumin**
¼ tsp.	**ground coriander**

1. Place all ingredients in blender (or food processor); cover. Blend until smooth.

2. Place sauce in large skillet. Heat over medium heat, stirring frequently, for 4 to 5 minutes, or until hot.

NUTRITIONAL INFORMATION (per serving): Calories: 90
Total Fat: 8 g   Saturated Fat: 0 g   Cholesterol: 0 mg   Sodium: 166 mg   Carbohydrates: 3 g   Fiber: 1 g   Sugars: 0 g   Protein: 5 g

Recipes containing the (GF) icon are designed to be gluten-free, but please read product labels for each ingredient to ensure this to be the case.

BREAKFAST

BANANA OAT PANCAKES

SERVES: 8 (2 pancakes each)   Prep Time: 15 min.   Cooking Time: 16 min.

CONTAINER EQUIVALENTS (per serving): 1 ½

1 cup	**unsweetened almond milk**
2	**large eggs**
1	**large ripe banana**
1 tsp.	**pure vanilla extract**
1 tsp.	**baking powder, gluten-free**
½ tsp.	**ground cinnamon**
1 dash	**sea salt (or Himalayan salt)**
2 cups	**dry old-fashioned rolled oats, gluten-free**
½ tsp.	**extra-virgin organic coconut oil**
3 cups	**fresh mixed berries**

1. Place almond milk, eggs, banana, extract, baking powder, cinnamon, salt, and oats in blender; cover. Blend until smooth.

2. Heat oil in nonstick skillet over medium-low heat.

3. Pour ¼ cup batter onto the skillet; cook for 2 to 3 minutes, or until bubbles form around the edges of the pancake. Flip with spatula; cook for an additional 90 seconds.

4. Continue with remaining batter.

5. Serve with fresh berries.

TIPS:

- If you want to make sure these pancakes are gluten-free, look for certified gluten-free oats. Oats are a naturally gluten-free food, however they are easily contaminated with gluten during harvesting. Therefore, to ensure you have a gluten-free product, look for the gluten-free variety.

- Leftover pancakes can be reheated in a toaster.

NUTRITIONAL INFORMATION (per serving): Calories: 137
Total Fat: 3 g   Saturated Fat: 1 g   Cholesterol: 47 mg   Sodium: 139 mg   Carbohydrates: 22 g   Fiber: 4 g   Sugars: 5 g   Protein: 5 g

CHOCOLATE PROTEIN CREPES

SERVES: 4 (1 crepe each)   Prep Time: 15 min.   Cooking Time: 12 min.

CONTAINER EQUIVALENTS (per serving): ½   1

7 to 8	**large egg whites (1 cup)**
1 scoop	**whey protein powder, chocolate flavor**
	Nonstick cooking spray
1 cup	**reduced fat (2%) plain Greek yogurt**
½ tsp.	**pure vanilla extract**
	Stevia (to taste; optional)
1 cup	**sliced strawberries**
1 cup	**fresh blueberries**

1. Combine egg whites and protein powder in a medium bowl; mix well.
2. Heat small nonstick skillet (or omelet pan), lightly coated with spray, on medium-high heat.
3. Spoon about ¼ cup batter into skillet; cook for 1 to 2 minutes, or until bubbles form on top. Flip with spatula and cook for 30 seconds.
4. Repeat with remaining batter to make four crepes. Set aside.
5. Combine yogurt, extract, and stevia (if desired) in a small bowl; mix well.
6. Fill crepes evenly with yogurt mixture, strawberries, and blueberries.

TIP:

Avoid substituting other protein powders for whey. It may affect the consistency of the batter.

NUTRITIONAL INFORMATION (per serving): Calories: 131
Total Fat: 1 g   Saturated Fat: 1 g   Cholesterol: 9 mg   Sodium: 128 mg   Carbohydrates: 12 g   Fiber: 2 g   Sugars: 9 g   Protein: 17 g

HEALTHY FRENCH TOAST

SERVES: 2   Prep Time: 10 min.   Cooking Time: 6 min.

CONTAINER EQUIVALENTS (per serving): ⬜ 1 🟥 ½ 🟥 ½ 🥄 ½

2	large eggs
2 Tbsp.	unsweetened almond milk
2 tsp.	pure maple syrup (or raw honey), *divided use*
½ tsp.	ground cinnamon
2 slices	low-sodium sprouted whole-grain bread
1 tsp.	extra-virgin organic coconut oil
1 cup	fresh sliced strawberries

1. Combine eggs, almond milk, *1 tsp.* maple syrup, and cinnamon in a shallow pan; whisk to blend.
2. Soak each slice of bread in egg mixture for 5 minutes, turning halfway.
3. Heat oil in medium nonstick skillet over medium heat.
4. Add bread; cook for 2 to 3 minutes on each side, or until golden brown.
5. Top each slice evenly with strawberries and *remaining 1 tsp.* maple syrup.
6. Serve immediately.

VARIATIONS:

If strawberries are not in season, serve French toast with:

- apples, chopped and cinnamon
- vanilla-infused peaches
- ¼ large banana, chopped
- mangoes, chopped

NUTRITIONAL INFORMATION (per serving): Calories: 219
Total Fat: 8 g   Saturated Fat: 4 g   Cholesterol: 186 mg   Sodium: 84 mg   Carbohydrates: 27 g   Fiber: 5 g   Sugars: 8 g   Protein: 11 g

OVEN-FRIED CHICKEN AND WAFFLES

SERVES: 4   Prep Time: 30 min.   Cooking Time: 36 min.

CONTAINER EQUIVALENTS (per serving): ⬜ 1 ⬛ 1½ ⬛ ½ ⬛ ½ 🥄 1

2 Tbsp.	pine nuts, toasted
1 Tbsp.	cornmeal
½ tsp.	onion powder
½ tsp.	ground paprika
½ tsp.	garlic powder
½ tsp.	ground black pepper
¼ tsp.	ground cayenne pepper
½ tsp.	dried oregano leaves
½ tsp.	dried thyme leaves
¼ tsp.	sea salt (or Himalayan salt)
½ tsp.	baking powder, gluten-free
¼ cup	almond flour
¼ cup	coconut flour
2 Tbsp.	grated parmigiano cheese
½ cup	low-fat buttermilk
1	large egg white (2 Tbsp.)
4 (4-oz.) ea.	raw chicken breasts, boneless, skinless
1 Tbsp.	olive oil

1. Preheat oven to 425° F.

2. Place pine nuts and cornmeal in food processor (or blender); cover. Pulse until finely ground.

3. Combine pine nut mixture, onion powder, paprika, garlic powder, black pepper, cayenne pepper, oregano, thyme, salt, baking powder, almond flour, coconut flour, and cheese in a shallow dish; mix well. Set aside.

4. Combine buttermilk and egg white in a shallow dish; whisk to blend.

5. Dip each chicken breast into the buttermilk mixture; dredge in pine nut mixture until evenly coated. Set aside.

6. Heat oil in large, ovenproof skillet over medium-high heat until fragrant.

7. Add chicken breasts; cook for 3 to 4 minutes. Turn chicken.

8. Place skillet in oven; bake for 10 to 12 minutes, or until a thermometer inserted into the thickest part of each breast reads 165° F. Set aside.

WAFFLES recipe on the following page.

NUTRITIONAL INFORMATION including Waffles (per serving): Calories: 427
Total Fat: 19 g   Saturated Fat: 4 g   Cholesterol: 77 mg   Sodium: 767 mg   Carbohydrates: 30 g   Fiber: 6 g   Sugars: 7 g   Protein: 37 g

WAFFLES

SERVES: 12 (1 waffle each)   Prep Time: 30 min.   Cooking Time: 36 min.

CONTAINER EQUIVALENTS (per serving): ⬜ 1 🟦 ½

2 cups	**oat flour (grind raw oats in a blender or food processor to make flour)**
2 Tbsp.	**ground flaxseeds**
¾ cup	**whey protein powder, vanilla flavor**
1 tsp.	**baking powder, gluten-free**
1 tsp.	**pure vanilla extract**
2 cups	**unsweetened almond milk**
4	**large egg whites (½ cup), beaten to form stiff peaks**
1 pinch	**sea salt (or Himalayan salt)**
	Nonstick cooking spray
12 tsp.	**pure maple syrup (1 tsp. per waffle)**

1. Preheat waffle iron.
2. Combine oat flour, flaxseeds, protein powder, and baking powder in a medium bowl; mix well. Set aside.
3. Combine extract and almond milk in a medium bowl; whisk to blend.
4. Add the flour mixture to the milk mixture; whisk gently just until a smooth batter forms.
5. Gently fold in egg whites and salt.
6. Cook ⅔ cup batter in preheated waffle iron, lightly coated with spray, for approximately 3 to 5 minutes (or according to specifications of your particular model), or until crisp and golden brown.
7. Place each waffle on a serving plate, top with one chicken breast, drizzle with maple syrup, and enjoy!

TIPS:

- I find it more efficient to make the waffles in larger batches, then freeze the leftovers and reheat them in the toaster. These ingredients should yield approximately 12 waffles, depending on the size of your iron.
- The key to light, crispy waffles is to use the Belgian technique. Beat your egg whites to form stiff peaks in a separate bowl; fold them into the batter just before cooking.
- This recipe by itself is considered to be vegetarian 🟢.
- Avoid substituting other protein powders for whey. It may affect the consistency of the batter.

NUTRITIONAL INFORMATION Waffles only (per serving): Calories: 137
Total Fat: 3 g   Saturated Fat: 1 g   Cholesterol: 7 mg   Sodium: 103 mg   Carbohydrates: 19 g   Fiber: 2 g   Sugars: 5 g   Protein: 8 g

PANCAKES WITH BLUEBERRY JAM

SERVES: 7 (2 pancakes each)   Prep Time: 15 min.   Cooking Time: 14 min.

CONTAINER EQUIVALENTS (per serving): ▢ 1   ⬤—— 2½

1½ cups	**all-purpose gluten-free flour**
3 tsp.	**baking powder, gluten-free**
1 dash	**sea salt (or Himalayan salt)**
1½ cups	**unsweetened almond milk**
1	**large egg**
1 Tbsp.	**pure maple syrup (or raw honey)**
5 Tbsp.	**organic grass-fed butter, melted**
1 tsp.	**pure vanilla extract**
7 Tbsp.	**Blueberry Jam (recipe, pg. 77)**

1. Combine flour, baking powder, and salt in a small bowl; mix well. Set aside.

2. Combine almond milk, egg, maple syrup, butter, and extract in a medium bowl; whisk to blend.

3. Add flour mixture to almond milk mixture; whisk to blend until there are no lumps.

4. Heat large nonstick skillet over medium heat.

5. Pour ¼ cup batter onto the skillet; cook for 2 to 3 minutes, or until bubbles form around the edges of the pancake. Flip with spatula; cook for an additional 90 seconds.

6. Continue with remaining batter.

7. Serve 2 pancakes with 1 Tbsp. Blueberry Jam for each serving.

TIPS:

- If pancakes are too thick, add some additional almond milk.

- Leftover pancakes can be reheated in the toaster.

NUTRITIONAL INFORMATION (per serving): Calories: 199
Total Fat: 11 g   Saturated Fat: 5 g   Cholesterol: 48 mg   Sodium: 274 mg   Carbohydrates: 23 g   Fiber: 3 g   Sugars: 4 g   Protein: 4 g

Recipes containing the **GF** icon are designed to be gluten-free, but please read product labels for each ingredient to ensure this to be the case.

PEANUT BUTTER AND CHOCOLATE STEEL-CUT OATMEAL

SERVES: 4 (approx. ½ cup cooked each)   Prep Time: 10 min.   Cooking Time: 30 min.

CONTAINER EQUIVALENTS (per serving): 1½   ½   ●—1

4 cups	**water**
¼ tsp.	**sea salt (or Himalayan salt)**
1 cup	**dry steel-cut oats, gluten-free**
1½ scoops	**Chocolate Vegan Shakeology®**
½ tsp.	**pure caramel extract, vegan**
4 tsp.	**all-natural peanut butter**
¼ tsp.	**ground cinnamon**
8 Tbsp.	**fresh mixed berries (2 Tbsp. per serving)**

1. Bring water and salt to a boil in medium saucepan over medium-high heat.
2. Add oats; mix well. Reduce heat to low. Gently boil, stirring occasionally, for 20 to 30 minutes, or until thick and soft. Remove from heat.
3. Add Shakeology, extract, and peanut butter; mix well.
4. Top evenly with cinnamon and berries to serve.

TIP:

Caramel extract can be found at specialty stores or online. Look for an all-natural product.

NUTRITIONAL INFORMATION (per serving): Calories: 258
Total Fat: 7 g   Saturated Fat: 1 g   Cholesterol: 0 mg   Sodium: 268 mg   Carbohydrates: 38 g   Fiber: 7 g   Sugars: 6 g   Protein: 12 g

POACHED EGGS WITH ASPARAGUS TOAST

SERVES: 2   Prep Time: 10 min.   Cooking Time: 10 min.

CONTAINER EQUIVALENTS (per serving): ½   1   ½   ½

½ tsp.	olive oil
10	medium asparagus spears, steamed
2 cups	hot water
1 tsp.	fresh lemon juice
2	large eggs
2 slices	low-sodium sprouted whole-grain bread, toasted
2 Tbsp.	Lemon Garlic Sauce (recipe, pg. 87)
	Freshly ground black pepper (to taste; optional)

1. Heat oil in medium nonstick skillet over medium heat.

2. Add asparagus; cook for 3 to 5 minutes, turning occasionally, or until tender-crisp. Set aside.

3. Bring water to a boil in medium saucepan over medium-high heat. Add lemon juice; reduce heat to maintain a gentle boil.

4. Place one egg into a small bowl. Hold bowl close to the water's surface and slip the egg into the water, repeat with remaining egg; cook for about 3 to 4 minutes, or until whites are completely set. Gently lift eggs out of water.

5. Spread each piece of toast with Lemon Garlic Sauce. Top with five asparagus spears, one egg, and pepper (if desired).

6. Serve immediately.

NUTRITIONAL INFORMATION (per serving): Calories: 224
Total Fat: 11 g   Saturated Fat: 2 g   Cholesterol: 204 mg   Sodium: 181 mg   Carbohydrates: 20 g   Fiber: 5 g   Sugars: 2 g   Protein: 12 g

PORTABELLO MUSHROOM AND GOAT CHEESE OMELET

SERVES: 1   Prep Time: 15 min.   Cooking Time: 8 min.

CONTAINER EQUIVALENTS (per serving): ■ 1 ■ 1 ■ ½ ●—1

2	large eggs
2 Tbsp.	water (or unsweetened almond milk)
¼ tsp.	sea salt (or Himalayan salt)
1 dash	ground black pepper
1 tsp.	olive oil, *divided use*
1 cup	thinly sliced baby portabello (or button) mushrooms
4½ tsp.	crumbled goat cheese
	Chopped fresh flat leaf (Italian) parsley (for garnish; optional)

1. Combine eggs, water, salt, and pepper in a medium bowl; whisk to blend. Set aside.

2. Heat *½ tsp.* oil in medium skillet over medium-low heat.

3. Add mushrooms; cook, stirring frequently, for 5 minutes, or until tender. Remove mushrooms from pan. Set aside.

4. Heat *remaining ½ tsp.* oil in same skillet over medium-low heat.

5. Add eggs. Do not stir. As eggs set, lift edges, letting uncooked portion flow underneath.

6. When eggs are almost set add mushrooms and cheese. Cook for 1 to 2 minutes, or until heated through. Gently fold in half.

7. Serve omelet immediately; garnish with parsley (if desired).

VARIATIONS:
(Other good omelet combinations include)

- Red bell peppers and grated Parmesan cheese
- Spinach and feta cheese
- Broccoli and cheddar cheese
- Asparagus and provolone cheese

NUTRITIONAL INFORMATION (per serving): Calories: 235
Total Fat: 17 g   Saturated Fat: 6 g   Cholesterol: 378 mg   Sodium: 771 mg   Carbohydrates: 3 g   Fiber: 1 g   Sugars: 2 g   Protein: 17 g

Recipes containing the (GF) icon are designed to be gluten-free, but please read product labels for each ingredient to ensure this to be the case.

STUFFED CREPE WITH HEALTHIER HOLLANDAISE SAUCE

SERVES: 1   Prep Time: 15 min.   Cooking Time: 28 min.

CONTAINER EQUIVALENTS (per serving): ■ 2 ■ 1½ ■ 1 ●— 1½

CREPE FILLING:

2 oz.	raw chicken breast, boneless, skinless, cut into 1-inch cubes
½ tsp.	chopped fresh thyme
1 tsp.	chopped fresh dill weed
½ tsp.	ground chili powder
	Sea salt (or Himalayan salt) and ground black pepper (to taste; optional)
1 tsp.	olive oil
¼	medium onion, chopped
½	medium red bell pepper, chopped
4	cremini (or brown or button) mushrooms, sliced thin
4	medium asparagus spears, chopped
1	medium tomato, chopped
2 Tbsp.	dry white wine (or water)

CREPE:

½ tsp.	olive oil
2	large eggs, beaten
2 Tbsp.	Healthier Hollandaise Sauce (recipe, pg. 83)

CREPE FILLING:

1. Evenly sprinkle chicken with thyme, dill, chili powder, salt (if desired), and pepper (if desired). Set aside.
2. Heat oil in large skillet over medium-high heat.
3. Add chicken; cook, stirring frequently, for 5 to 7 minutes, or until chicken is no longer pink in the middle. Remove from pan. Keep warm.
4. Add onion and bell pepper to skillet; cook, stirring occasionally, for 5 to 6 minutes, or until onion is translucent.
5. Add mushrooms; cook, stirring frequently, for 5 to 6 minutes, or until mushrooms release their liquid.
6. Add asparagus and tomato; cook, stirring frequently, for 2 to 3 minutes.
7. Add wine; cook, stirring constantly, for 2 to 3 minutes, or until liquid has evaporated.
8. Remove from heat. Set aside.

CREPE:

1. Heat oil in nonstick omelet (or crepe pan) over medium-high heat.
2. Add eggs. Swirl pan continuously so that a thin, even layer of egg covers the pan. Do not stir. Cook for 2 to 3 minutes, or until eggs are cooked through.
3. Carefully slide crepe onto a serving dish. Top with chicken mixture. Fold each side of crepe to the middle.
4. Top with Healthier Hollandaise Sauce.

NUTRITIONAL INFORMATION (per serving): Calories: 460
Total Fat: 27 g   Saturated Fat: 9 g   Cholesterol: 461 mg   Sodium: 735 mg   Carbohydrates: 20 g   Fiber: 6 g   Sugars: 11 g   Protein: 31 g

Recipes containing the GF icon are designed to be gluten-free, but please read product labels for each ingredient to ensure this to be the case.

SWISS OATMEAL

SERVES: 1   Prep Time: 10 min.   Cooking Time: None

CONTAINER EQUIVALENTS (per serving): ◻ 1 ■ 1 ■ 1 ■ 1

¼ cup	**dry old-fashioned rolled oats, gluten-free**
¾ cup	**unsweetened almond milk, *divided use***
¾ cup	**reduced fat (2%) plain yogurt**
½ tsp.	**pure vanilla extract**
½ tsp.	**ground cinnamon**
½ cup	**chopped strawberries**
¼	**medium banana, chopped**
12	**raw almonds, chopped**
	Stevia (to taste; optional)

1. Place oats, *½ cup* almond milk, yogurt, extract, and cinnamon in a medium bowl; mix well. Soak, covered, in the refrigerator overnight.

2. In the morning, add *remaining ¼ cup* almond milk; mix well.

3. Top with strawberries, banana, and almonds. Sprinkle stevia (if desired) over the top.

NUTRITIONAL INFORMATION (per serving): Calories: 379
Total Fat: 14 g   Saturated Fat: 3 g   Cholesterol: 9 mg   Sodium: 194 mg   Carbohydrates: 39 g   Fiber: 8 g   Sugars: 16 g   Protein: 24 g

Recipes containing the GF icon are designed to be gluten-free, but please read product labels for each ingredient to ensure this to be the case.

VANILLA PROTEIN PANCAKES WITH PEARS AND CINNAMON

SERVES: 5 (2 pancakes each)   Prep Time: 15 min.   Cooking Time: 15 min.

CONTAINER EQUIVALENTS (per serving): ⬤ ½ ⬤ ½ ⬤ 1 ⬤ 1

2 cups	**sliced pears**
1 tsp.	**ground cinnamon**
1 cup	**almond flour**
½ cup	**coconut flour**
½ cup	**unsweetened almond milk**
3	**large eggs**
1 tsp.	**pure vanilla extract**
1½ scoops	**whey protein powder, vanilla flavor**
	Nonstick cooking spray

1. Combine pears and cinnamon in a medium bowl; mix well. Set aside.
2. Combine almond flour and coconut flour in a medium bowl; mix well. Set aside.
3. Place almond milk, eggs, extract, and protein powder in blender; cover. Blend until smooth. Place in a large bowl.
4. Add almond flour mixture to almond milk mixture; mix well.
5. Heat medium nonstick skillet, lightly coated with spray, over medium-low heat.
6. Pour ¼ cup batter onto the skillet; cook for 2 to 3 minutes, or until edges start to set. Completely loosen pancake from skillet. Flip with spatula; cook for an additional 90 seconds.
7. Continue with remaining batter.
8. Serve topped evenly with pear and cinnamon mixture.

TIPS:

- Leftover pancakes can be reheated in the toaster.
- Avoid substituting other protein powders for whey. It may affect the consistency of the batter.

VARIATION:

Substitute chocolate protein powder for vanilla protein powder and ½ sliced large banana for pears.

RECIPE NOTE:

Normally, pancakes count as a yellow container, but since the protein powder along with the almond and coconut flours replace traditional flours, there's more protein and (healthy) fat in this recipe and less carbs.

NUTRITIONAL INFORMATION (per serving): Calories: 292
Total Fat: 16 g   Saturated Fat: 3 g   Cholesterol: 122 mg   Sodium: 81 mg   Carbohydrates: 24 g   Fiber: 10 g   Sugars: 7 g   Protein: 16 g

VEGETABLE EGG CUPS

SERVES: 6 (2 each)   Prep Time: 15 min.   Cooking Time: 20 min.

CONTAINER EQUIVALENTS (per serving): █ 1

	Nonstick cooking spray
12	large eggs
	Sea salt (or Himalayan salt) and ground black pepper (to taste; optional)
1 cup	chopped mushrooms
1	medium red bell pepper, finely chopped
2	green onions, thinly sliced
12 Tbsp.	Homemade Salsa (recipe, pg. 85)

1. Heat oven to 375° F.
2. Lightly coat a twelve-cup muffin tin with spray.
3. Place eggs in a large bowl; whisk to blend. Season with salt and pepper (if desired).
4. Add mushrooms, bell pepper, and green onions; mix well.
5. Evenly pour egg mixture into muffin cups.
6. Bake for 15 to 20 minutes, or until a toothpick inserted into the center of cups comes out clean.
7. Top each egg cup with 1 Tbsp. Homemade Salsa.

VARIATIONS:
(Other good vegetable combinations include)

- Chopped broccoli florets and shredded carrots
- Chopped red, green, and yellow bell peppers
- Chopped bell peppers with chopped onions
- Spinach and chopped mushrooms

RECIPE NOTE:

There are a few veggies in this recipe, but not really enough to count as a full green. Your best bet is to enjoy this recipe as a great protein source and get your greens from a nice fresh salad!

NUTRITIONAL INFORMATION (per serving): Calories: 156
Total Fat: 10 g   Saturated Fat: 3 g   Cholesterol: 372 mg   Sodium: 228 mg   Carbohydrates: 3 g   Fiber: 1 g   Sugars: 2 g   Protein: 13 g

LUNCH

CALABRESE CHICKEN

SERVES: 1   Prep Time: 10 min.   Cooking Time: 10 min.

CONTAINER EQUIVALENTS (per serving):   ■ ½   ■ 1   ■ 1   ●— 1

1 (4-oz.)	**raw chicken breast, boneless, skinless**
1 dash	**ground black pepper**
½ tsp.	**olive oil**
1 serving	**Calabrese Salad (recipe, pg. 53), disassembled**
	Fresh basil leaves for garnish

1. Season both sides of chicken evenly with pepper.
2. Heat oil in medium nonstick skillet over medium heat.
3. Add chicken; cook for 3 to 4 minutes on each side, or until no longer pink in the middle.
4. Top chicken with slices of tomato and basil leaves from Calabrese Salad. Top with mozzarella slice (including pesto sauce).
5. Reduce heat to medium-low; cook, covered, for an additional 1 to 2 minutes, or until cheese is melted and tomatoes are softened.
6. Serve topped with fresh basil leaves.

NUTRITIONAL INFORMATION (per serving): Calories: 288
Total Fat: 13 g   Saturated Fat: 4 g   Cholesterol: 91 mg   Sodium: 719 mg   Carbohydrates: 7 g   Fiber: 1 g   Sugars: 5 g   Protein: 32 g

Recipes containing the GF icon are designed to be gluten-free, but please read product labels for each ingredient to ensure this to be the case.

CHICKEN PARMESAN

SERVES: 1   Prep Time: 15 min.   Cooking Time: 20 min.

CONTAINER EQUIVALENTS (per serving):   ■ 2   ■ 1½   ■ 1   ●— 1

1	**oven-fried chicken breast— left over from Oven-Fried Chicken and Waffles (recipe, pg. 101)**
3 Tbsp.	**Grandma's Tomato Sauce (recipe, pg. 81)**
1 Tbsp.	**shredded mozzarella cheese**
1 Tbsp.	**shredded Parmesan cheese**
1 cup	**mixed vegetables (like broccoli, carrots, cauliflower, or green beans), steamed**

1. Preheat oven to 350° F.
2. Place chicken in medium baking dish.
3. Top with Grandma's Tomato Sauce and cheeses.
4. Cover with aluminum foil. Bake for 15 to 20 minutes, or until cheese is bubbly and chicken is heated through.
5. Serve with vegetables.

VARIATIONS:
(substitute for mixed vegetables)

- One serving plain Zoodles (recipe, pg. 183).

- One serving spaghetti squash.

  To make spaghetti squash, place a medium spaghetti squash (about 3 lbs.) on a parchment-lined baking sheet. Poke the squash 2 or 3 times with a fork. Bake at 350° F. for 60 to 80 minutes. Cool for 20 to 30 minutes. Cut squash in half lengthwise. Remove seeds. Scrape flesh into stringy noodles. Serve four portions topped with basil.

NUTRITIONAL INFORMATION (per serving): Calories: 417
Total Fat: 20 g   Saturated Fat: 6 g   Cholesterol: 81 mg   Sodium: 984 mg   Carbohydrates: 23 g   Fiber: 7 g   Sugars: 9 g   Protein: 37 g

Recipes containing the GF icon are designed to be gluten-free, but please read product labels for each ingredient to ensure this to be the case.

CREAMY CHICKEN SALAD WRAP

SERVES: 1   Prep Time: 15 min.   Cooking Time: None

CONTAINER EQUIVALENTS (per serving): ■ 2   ■ 1½   ■ ½   ■ 1   ■ ½   ■ ½

1	**8-inch sprouted whole-grain tortilla**
1 Tbsp.	**Dijon mustard, gluten-free**
1 serving	**Creamy Chicken Salad (recipe, pg. 55), with 2 cups of the shredded romaine lettuce**

1. Spread tortilla with mustard if desired.
2. Place Creamy Chicken Salad and lettuce on tortilla.
3. Fold in the sides of the tortilla and roll the wrap burrito-style.

VARIATIONS:

Bread
(substitute for tortilla):

- 1 English muffin
- 1 6½-inch whole wheat pita
- 1 sprouted whole-grain bun (or roll)
- 1 small whole wheat bagel

Vegetables
(add any ½ cup combination of the following and add ½ green to container equivalents):

- Sliced red bell peppers
- Baby spinach
- Sliced zucchini
- Sliced red onions
- Sprouts
- Kale
- Cabbage
- Sliced radishes

NUTRITIONAL INFORMATION Creamy Chicken Salad Wrap only (per serving): Calories: 457
Total Fat: 15 g   Saturated Fat: 3 g   Cholesterol: 91 mg   Sodium: 816 mg   Carbohydrates: 41 g   Fiber: 7 g   Sugars: 12 g   Protein: 41 g

EASY PIZZA

SERVES: 1   Prep Time: 15 min.   Cooking Time: 10 min.

CONTAINER EQUIVALENTS (per serving): ■ 1   ▢ 1½   ■ 1

¼ cup	all-natural tomato sauce, no salt or sugar added	1. Preheat oven to 425° F.
¼ tsp.	dried oregano leaves	2. Combine tomato sauce, oregano, and garlic in a small bowl; mix well. Set aside.
½ clove	garlic, finely chopped	3. Place tortilla on a baking sheet; spread with tomato sauce.
1	8-inch sprouted whole wheat tortilla	4. Top with broccoli, mushrooms, and cheeses.
¼ cup	chopped steamed broccoli	5. Bake for 8 to 10 minutes, or until cheese is bubbly.
¼ cup	sliced mushrooms	6. Serve immediately.
2 Tbsp.	shredded mozzarella cheese	
2 Tbsp.	shredded Parmesan cheese	

VARIATIONS:

Bread
(substitute for tortilla):

- 1 English muffin
- 1 6½-inch whole wheat pita
- Store-bought whole wheat pizza dough (use ⅛ and follow package directions)

Substitute for vegetable toppings
(any ½ cup combination of the following):

- Sliced red bell peppers
- Baby spinach
- Sliced zucchini
- Asparagus
- Chopped red onions
- Grilled chopped eggplant

Substitute for cheese toppings
(any ¼ cup combination of the following):

- Crumbled feta cheese
- Crumbled goat cheese
- Crumbled blue cheese
- Shredded provolone cheese
- Shredded cheddar cheese
- Shredded jack cheese

Protein toppings
(add 1 red container equivalent):

- ¾ cup chopped cooked chicken breast
- ¾ cup cooked 93% lean ground turkey (or chicken)
- ¾ cup cooked shrimp
- 6 slices cooked chopped ham (or turkey)

Miscellaneous
(add 1 orange container equivalent):

- 10 medium pitted olives

NUTRITIONAL INFORMATION Easy Pizza only (per serving): Calories: 263
Total Fat: 10 g   Saturated Fat: 5 g   Cholesterol: 20 mg   Sodium: 591 mg   Carbohydrates: 29 g   Fiber: 4 g   Sugars: 5 g   Protein: 15 g

FRITTATA

SERVES: 6   Prep Time: 15 min.   Cooking Time: 10 min.

CONTAINER EQUIVALENTS (per serving): ■½ ■½ ■1 ■½

6	**large eggs, lightly beaten**
¼ tsp.	**sea salt (or Himalayan salt)**
½ cup	**shredded Parmesan cheese**
3 servings	**Chicken Stuffed Bell Peppers (recipe, pg. 147), coarsely chopped**
1 tsp.	**olive oil**
¼ cup	**chopped fresh flat leaf (Italian) parsley**

1. Preheat oven to broil.
2. Combine eggs, salt, and cheese in a large mixing bowl; whisk to blend.
3. Add chopped Chicken Stuffed Bell Peppers; mix well.
4. Heat oil in 12-inch nonstick oven-safe skillet over medium-low heat.
5. Pour egg mixture into skillet; cook, stirring frequently with rubber spatula, for 4 to 5 minutes, or until egg mixture has set on the bottom and begins to set on top.
6. Place skillet in oven. Broil for 3 to 4 minutes, or until lightly browned and fluffy.
7. Cut into 6 servings.
8. Sprinkle with parsley; serve immediately.

TIPS:

- Frittata can be made the evening before and stored in the refrigerator for up to 4 days in an airtight container.
- Heat one serving at a time on the stove top or in a microwave.
- Frittata is especially delicious served with a simple green salad drizzled with balsamic vinegar.

NUTRITIONAL INFORMATION Frittata only (per serving): Calories: 266
Total Fat: 12 g   Saturated Fat: 5 g   Cholesterol: 227 mg   Sodium: 602 mg   Carbohydrates: 15 g   Fiber: 3 g   Sugars: 3 g   Protein: 23 g

Recipes containing the GF icon are designed to be gluten-free, but please read product labels for each ingredient to ensure this to be the case.

MEXICAN TACO LETTUCE CUPS

SERVES: 1 Prep Time: 15 min.   Cooking Time: None

CONTAINER EQUIVALENTS (per serving): █ 1½ ▢ 1 █ 1½ █ 1 ●—1

4	**Bibb lettuce leaves**
1¼ cups	**Mexican Taco Meat (recipe, pg. 157), warm**
½ cup	**shredded carrots**
¼ cup	**black beans, warm**
¼ cup	**corn kernels, warm**
¼ cup	**Homemade Salsa (recipe, pg. 85)**
¼ cup	**shredded cheddar cheese**

1. Place lettuce leaves on a large serving plate.
2. Top evenly with Mexican Taco Meat, carrots, beans, corn, Homemade Salsa, and cheese. Enjoy!

VARIATIONS:
Substitute Boston lettuce or radicchio for Bibb lettuce

Vegetable toppings
(add any ½ cup combination of the following and add ½ green container equivalent):

- Shredded cabbage
- Chopped jicama
- Sliced red bell peppers

Cheese toppings
(substitute for cheddar cheese):

- Cotija
- Monterey jack
- Panela

NUTRITIONAL INFORMATION Mexican Taco Lettuce Cups only (per serving): Calories: 473
Total Fat: 21 g Saturated Fat: 9 g Cholesterol: 114 mg Sodium: 768 mg Carbohydrates: 37 g Fiber: 10 g Sugars: 10 g Protein: 37 g

Recipes containing the **GF** icon are designed to be gluten-free, but please read product labels for each ingredient to ensure this to be the case.

OPEN MEATBALL SUB

SERVES: 1   Prep Time: 15 min.   Cooking Time: 10 min.

CONTAINER EQUIVALENTS (per serving): ⬛ 1½ ⬜ 1 ⬛ 1 ⬛ 1 ⬤━ 1

½	**sprouted whole-grain roll**
1 serving	**Italian Meatballs (recipe, pg. 153), warm (approx. 4 meatballs)**
¼ cup	**Grandma's Tomato Sauce (recipe, pg. 81), warm**
2 Tbsp.	**shredded mozzarella cheese**
2 Tbsp.	**shredded Parmesan cheese**
	Chopped fresh flat leaf (Italian) parsley (for garnish; optional)

1. Preheat oven to 400° F.
2. Wrap bottom of roll with aluminum foil, leaving top exposed.
3. Top roll with Italian Meatballs.
4. Top evenly with Grandma's Tomato Sauce and cheeses.
5. Bake for 8 to 10 minutes, or until cheese is melted and bubbly.
6. Sprinkle with parsley (if desired) and enjoy!

RECIPE NOTE:

Please note that the green portions are coming from Grandma's Tomato Sauce, which is filled with healthy fiber without preservatives and additives like other canned tomato sauces.

NUTRITIONAL INFORMATION (per serving): Calories: 424
Total Fat: 21 g   Saturated Fat: 8 g   Cholesterol: 127 mg   Sodium: 801 mg   Carbohydrates: 25 g   Fiber: 4 g   Sugars: 8 g   Protein: 32 g

SEARED AHI TUNA RICE BOWL

SERVES: 1 Prep Time: 15 min. Cooking Time: 40 min.

CONTAINER EQUIVALENTS (per serving): ◻ 1 ◼ 1 ◻ ½

¼ cup	**dry medium grain brown rice, rinsed, drained (or ½ cup cooked rice)**
¾ cup	**water**
1 tsp.	**reduced-sodium tamari soy sauce, gluten-free**
1 Tbsp.	**rice vinegar**
1 serving	**Seared Ahi Tuna with Pumpkin Seed Sauce (recipe, pg. 163)**
1	**thinly sliced green onion (optional; for garnish)**

1. Combine rice and water in medium saucepan; bring to a boil over medium-high heat.

2. Reduce heat to low; gently boil, covered, for 35 to 40 minutes, or until water is absorbed. Remove from heat and let rice stand covered for 10 minutes.

3. Transfer rice to a serving bowl. Top with soy sauce and vinegar; toss gently, with a large spoon, to blend.

4. Top rice with Seared Ahi Tuna with Pumpkin Seed Sauce; garnish with green onion (if desired).

TIP:

- Remove veggies from Seared Ahi Tuna with Pumpkin Seed Sauce and Veggies recipe. You can eat the veggies as a snack.

- If using cooked rice, skip to step three.

NUTRITIONAL INFORMATION (per serving): Calories: 332
Total Fat: 4 g Saturated Fat: 0 g Cholesterol: 44 mg Sodium: 422 mg Carbohydrates: 39 g Fiber: 2 g Sugars: 2 g Protein: 33 g

Recipes containing the GF icon are designed to be gluten-free, but please read product labels for each ingredient to ensure this to be the case.

SHRIMP PANZANELLA

SERVES: 4 (approx. 2 cups each)   Prep Time: 20 min.   Cooking Time: 5 min.

CONTAINER EQUIVALENTS (per serving): ● 1 ○ 1 ■ 1 ▨ 1

1 tsp.	olive oil
4	waffles left over from Oven-Fried Chicken and Waffles (recipe, pg. 103), cut into 1-inch cubes
¼ tsp.	sea salt (or Himalayan salt)
2	medium heirloom tomatoes, cut into 1-inch pieces
1 cup	chopped red bell pepper
1 cup	chopped yellow bell pepper
1	medium hothouse cucumber, cut into 1-inch pieces
½ cup	sliced red onion
½ cup	chopped fresh basil leaves
¼ cup	Lemon Dijon Salad Dressing (recipe, pg. 75)
3 cups	cooked shrimp, peeled, deveined

1. Heat oil in large nonstick skillet over medium-high heat.

2. Add waffles and salt; cook, stirring frequently, for 5 minutes, or until browned and toasted. Set aside to cool.

3. Combine tomatoes, bell peppers, cucumber, onion, and basil in a large serving bowl; toss gently to blend.

4. Add cooled waffles and Lemon Dijon Salad Dressing; toss gently to blend.

5. Divide salad evenly between four salad plates. Top each salad with ¾ cup shrimp.

6. Serve immediately.

NUTRITIONAL INFORMATION (per serving): Calories: 346
Total Fat: 11 g Saturated Fat: 2 g Cholesterol: 234 mg Sodium: 574 mg Carbohydrates: 29 g Fiber: 5 g Sugars: 10 g Protein: 33 g

TUNA SALAD SANDWICH

SERVES: 1   Prep Time: 15 min.   Cooking Time: None

CONTAINER EQUIVALENTS (per serving):   ■ 1   ▢ 2   ■ 1   ●━ ½

1	**sprouted whole-grain bun, cut in half lengthwise**
2 Tbsp.	**hot pepper sauce (optional)**
1 serving	**Tuna Salad (recipe, pg. 71)**
1	**large lettuce leaf**
2 slices	**medium tomato**
¼ cup	**sliced cucumber**

1. Spread both sides of bun with hot sauce (if desired).
2. Spread Tuna Salad on bottom half of bun.
3. Top Tuna Salad with lettuce, tomato, cucumber, and top half of bun.
4. Serve immediately.

VARIATIONS:

Bread
(substitute for roll):

- 1 English muffin
- 1 6½-inch whole wheat pita
- 1 8-inch sprouted whole-grain tortilla
- 1 small whole wheat bagel

For vegetables:
(substitute or add any ½ cup combination of the following and add ½ green container equivalents for every additional ½ cup added):

- Sliced red bell peppers
- Baby spinach
- Sliced zucchini
- Sliced red onions
- Sprouts
- Kale
- Cabbage
- Sliced radishes

NUTRITIONAL INFORMATION Tuna Salad Sandwich only (per serving): Calories: 379
Total Fat:10 g   Saturated Fat: 2 g   Cholesterol: 38 mg   Sodium: 672 mg   Carbohydrates: 40 g   Fiber: 7 g   Sugars: 6 g   Protein: 34 g

DINNER

BEEF STEW WITH SWEET POTATOES

SERVES: 6 (approx. 2 cups each)   Prep Time: 20 min.   Cooking Time: 2 hrs. 56 min.

CONTAINER EQUIVALENTS (per serving): ▢ ½   ▢ ½   ▢ 1½

1 tsp.	olive oil
1 lb. 10 oz.	raw lean beef stew meat
1	medium onion, chopped
1	medium carrot, sliced
2	medium celery stalks, chopped
4 cloves	garlic, finely chopped
8 cups	low-sodium organic beef broth, *divided use*
½ cup	red wine
¼ tsp.	sea salt (or Himalayan salt)
1 tsp.	ground black pepper
1 tsp.	ground smoked paprika
3	bay leaves
2	medium tomatoes, chopped
2	large sweet potatoes, cut into 1-inch cubes
2 tsp.	cornstarch, gluten-free (preferably GMO-free) (or arrowroot)
2 Tbsp.	lukewarm (tepid) water

1. Heat oil in large saucepan over medium-high heat.

2. Add stew meat; cook, stirring frequently, for 4 to 5 minutes, or until browned.

3. Add onion, carrot, and celery; cook, stirring occasionally, for 5 to 6 minutes, or until onion is translucent.

4. Add garlic; cook, stirring frequently, for 1 minute.

5. Add *1 cup* broth and wine; cook, stirring constantly, scraping bottom of pan so beef doesn't stick, for 5 to 8 minutes, or until liquid is reduced in half.

6. Add salt, pepper, paprika, bay leaves, and tomatoes. Bring to a boil. Reduce heat; gently boil, stirring occasionally, for 5 to 8 minutes, or until liquid has almost completely evaporated, and tomatoes begin to break down.

7. Add *remaining 7 cups* broth. Bring to a boil over medium-high heat. Reduce heat; gently boil, stirring occasionally, for 2 hours.

8. Add sweet potatoes; cook, stirring occasionally, for 10 to 15 minutes, or until sweet potatoes are tender.

9. Combine cornstarch and water in a small bowl; whisk to blend.

10. Add cornstarch mixture to stew; cook, stirring constantly, for 2 to 3 minutes, or until stew has thickened slightly.

NUTRITIONAL INFORMATION (per serving): Calories: 283
Total Fat: 9 g   Saturated Fat: 4 g   Cholesterol: 87 mg   Sodium: 434 mg   Carbohydrates: 17 g   Fiber: 3 g   Sugars: 6 g   Protein: 32 g

Recipes containing the GF icon are designed to be gluten-free, but please read product labels for each ingredient to ensure this to be the case.

CHICKEN STUFFED BELL PEPPERS

GF

SERVES: 8 (½ pepper each)   Prep Time: 20 min.   Cooking Time: 54 min.

CONTAINER EQUIVALENTS (per serving): ■ 1   ▢ 1   ■ 1   ■ ½

This is another one of my grandma's recipes. It's basically a meatball stuffed in a pepper.
But, it's a really fun, easy, and different way to get both your protein and vegetables all in one meal.

4	medium red (or yellow, orange, or green) bell peppers, cut in half, seeds removed
2 tsp.	olive oil
1	medium onion, chopped
2 cloves	garlic, finely chopped
1½ lbs.	raw chicken breast, boneless, skinless, chopped into ¾-inch pieces
1½ tsp.	ground chili powder
1½ tsp.	ground cumin
1 tsp.	sea salt (or Himalayan salt)
¼ tsp.	ground black pepper
1 cup	all-natural tomato sauce, no salt or sugar added
2 cups	cooked quinoa
1 cup	canned black beans, drained, rinsed
1 cup	frozen corn kernels
5 Tbsp.	chopped fresh cilantro, reserve some for garnish
2 Tbsp.	fresh lime juice
1 cup	shredded Monterey jack cheese
	Hot pepper sauce (to taste; optional)

1. Preheat oven to 375° F.
2. Place bell peppers, skin side down, in large baking dish; set aside.
3. Heat oil in large nonstick skillet over medium heat.
4. Add onion; cook, stirring frequently, for 4 to 5 minutes, or until onion is translucent.
5. Add garlic; cook, stirring frequently, for 1 minute.
6. Add chicken, chili powder, cumin, salt, and pepper; cook, stirring frequently, for 5 minutes, or until chicken is no longer pink.
7. Add tomato sauce, quinoa, beans, corn, cilantro, and lime juice. Reduce heat to medium-low; cook, stirring occasionally, for 3 to 5 minutes, or until heated through.
8. Divide chicken mixture evenly between pepper halves; cover lightly with foil.
9. Bake for 35 minutes, or until peppers are tender; remove foil.
10. Top each pepper evenly with cheese. Bake for 3 to 5 minutes, or until cheese is melted.
11. Serve sprinkled with cilantro and hot sauce (if desired).

NUTRITIONAL INFORMATION (per serving): Calories: 301
Total Fat: 9 g   Saturated Fat: 3 g   Cholesterol: 67 mg   Sodium: 614 mg   Carbohydrates: 28 g   Fiber: 6 g   Sugars: 5 g   Protein: 27 g

Recipes containing the GF icon are designed to be gluten-free, but please read product labels for each ingredient to ensure this to be the case.

14

CIOPPINO

SERVES: 6   Prep Time: 15 min.   Cooking Time: 1 hr.

CONTAINER EQUIVALENTS (per serving): ⬛ 2   ⬛ 1½

Christmas Eve dinner always meant the same thing in the Calabrese family: a huge, Italian fish dinner.
I loved going to the fish market with my grandma the day before to pick everything out: mussels (my favorite!),
clams, shrimp, crab legs, escargot, and eel. The beauty of this cioppino is that it works with any of your
favorite seafood. You don't need to wait until Christmas to feast on this delicious soup!

2 tsp.	**olive oil**
1	**medium onion, chopped**
1	**fennel bulb, finely chop fronds and reserve separately, thinly slice bulb**
5 cloves	**garlic, finely chopped**
½ tsp.	**ground black pepper**
½ tsp.	**ground white pepper**
3	**bay leaves**
1 cup	**dry white wine**
1 (28-oz.) can	**whole peeled tomatoes, crushed or chopped, no salt added**
8 cups	**seafood stock or broth (or 6 cups low-sodium vegetable broth and 2 cups clam juice)**
1 lb.	**raw clams, in shells**
1 lb.	**raw blue mussels, in shells**
1 lb.	**raw shrimp, peeled, deveined**
1 lb.	**raw tilapia fillets, cut into 1-inch chunks**
½ cup	**fresh basil leaves, finely chopped**

1. Heat oil in large saucepan over medium-high heat.
2. Add onion and sliced fennel bulb; cook, stirring occasionally, for 5 to 6 minutes, or until onion is translucent.
3. Add garlic; cook, stirring frequently, for 1 minute.
4. Add peppers, bay leaves, and wine. Bring to a boil. Reduce heat; gently boil, stirring occasionally, for 10 to 11 minutes, or until liquid has almost completely evaporated.
5. Add tomatoes. Bring to a boil over medium-high heat. Reduce heat; gently boil, stirring occasionally, for 10 to 12 minutes, or until two-thirds of liquid is remaining.
6. Add broth. Bring to a boil. Reduce heat; gently boil, stirring occasionally, for 25 to 30 minutes.
7. Add clams and mussels; cook, covered, for 5 to 10 minutes, or until clams and mussels begin to open.
8. Add shrimp and tilapia; cook, covered, for 2 to 3 minutes, or until all clams and mussels are open, shrimp is opaque, and tilapia flakes easily when tested with a fork. Discard any unopened clams or mussels. Discard bay leaves. Remove from heat.
9. Evenly divide between six serving bowls; evenly top with basil and chopped fennel fronds.

NUTRITIONAL INFORMATION (per serving): Calories: 303
Total Fat: 7 g   Saturated Fat: 1 g   Cholesterol: 134 mg   Sodium: 1,428 mg   Carbohydrates: 15 g   Fiber: 3 g   Sugars: 5 g   Protein: 39 g

Recipes containing the (GF) icon are designed to be gluten-free, but please read product labels for each ingredient to ensure this to be the case.

EGGPLANT TURKEY BURGER

SERVES: 4   Prep Time: 20 min.   Cooking Time: 16 min.

CONTAINER EQUIVALENTS (per serving): ■ 1½ ■ 1 ■ 1

12 oz.	**raw ground 93% lean turkey breast**
¾	**medium onion, ¼ finely chopped, ½ sliced, _divided use_**
2	**large egg whites (¼ cup)**
1 Tbsp.	**finely chopped fresh parsley**
1 tsp.	**hot pepper sauce (like Tabasco)**
1	**medium eggplant, peeled, sliced into 8 rounds**
1	**medium bell pepper, sliced (or chopped)**
1 tsp.	**olive oil**
4 slices	**Muenster cheese (4 oz.)**
1 Tbsp.	**balsamic vinegar**

1. Preheat grill or broiler to high.
2. Combine turkey, _chopped onion,_ egg whites, parsley, and hot sauce in a medium bowl; mix well. Form turkey into four patties.
3. Grill or broil patties for about 4 to 5 minutes on each side, or until no longer pink in the middle. Set aside. Keep warm.
4. Brush _sliced onion,_ eggplant, and bell pepper with oil.
5. Grill or broil for 2 to 3 minutes on each side, or until lightly browned.
6. Place a slice of eggplant on each of four serving plates. Top each with a patty, a slice of onion, a slice of bell pepper, and a slice of cheese. Sprinkle with vinegar and top with a second slice of eggplant.

NUTRITIONAL INFORMATION (per serving): Calories: 296
Total Fat: 17 g   Saturated Fat: 7 g   Cholesterol: 90 mg   Sodium: 277 mg   Carbohydrates: 11 g   Fiber: 5 g   Sugars: 5 g   Protein: 26 g

Recipes containing the GF icon are designed to be gluten-free, but please read product labels for each ingredient to ensure this to be the case.

ITALIAN MEATBALLS WITH GRANDMA'S TOMATO SAUCE

SERVES: 10 (approx. 4 meatballs each)   Prep Time: 30 min.   Cooking Time: 25 min.
CONTAINER EQUIVALENTS (per serving): ■ 2   ■ 1   ●—1

When I was a kid, everything was from scratch. The sauce took about 4–5 hours to cook properly and the meatballs were hand-rolled by Gram. We always said that no one else's tasted quite like hers—we joked that it must have been the olive oil naturally in my grandma's body that came out in her hands!

	Nonstick cooking spray
⅓ cup	**whole wheat bread crumbs**
¼ cup	**reduced fat (2%) milk (or unsweetened almond milk)**
2 tsp.	**olive oil**
1	**medium onion, finely chopped**
3 cloves	**garlic, finely chopped**
2 lbs.	**raw ground 93% lean ground turkey breast**
2	**large eggs**
¼ cup	**finely chopped fresh parsley**
2 Tbsp.	**grated Parmesan cheese**
1 tsp.	**dried oregano leaves**
½ tsp.	**sea salt (or Himalayan salt)**
½ tsp.	**ground black pepper**
4 cups	**Grandma's Tomato Sauce (recipe, pg. 81), warm**

1. Preheat oven to 425° F.
2. Line large baking sheet with parchment paper, lightly coated with spray.
3. Place bread crumbs and milk in a small bowl. Set aside; soak for 10 minutes.
4. Heat oil in medium skillet over medium-low heat.
5. Add onion; cook, stirring frequently, for 5 to 6 minutes, or until onion is translucent.
6. Add garlic; cook, stirring frequently, for 1 minute.
7. Combine onion mixture, turkey, eggs, parsley, cheese, oregano, salt, pepper, and bread crumb mixture in a large bowl; mix well with clean hands or wooden spoon. Refrigerate, covered, for 1 hour.
8. With clean wet hands, form turkey mixture into approximately 42 1-inch meatballs; arrange onto prepared baking sheet.
9. Bake for 13 to 18 minutes, or until browned and cooked through.
10. Serve topped with Grandma's Tomato Sauce.

SERVING SUGGESTIONS:
For one serving of Italian Meatballs

- Serve Italian Meatballs over 1 cup plain Zoodles (recipe, pg. 183)
  CONTAINER EQUIVALENTS (per serving): ■ 3   ■ 1   ●—1
- Serve Italian Meatballs over ½ cup cooked whole wheat (or quinoa) pasta
  CONTAINER EQUIVALENTS (per serving): ■ 2   ▢ 1   ■ 1   ●—1
- Serve Italian Meatballs in 2 large romaine lettuce leaves
  CONTAINER EQUIVALENTS (per serving): ■ 2½   ■ 1   ●—1

NUTRITIONAL INFORMATION Italian Meatballs with Sauce only (per serving): Calories: 276
Total Fat: 13 g   Saturated Fat: 4 g   Cholesterol: 110 mg   Sodium: 500 mg   Carbohydrates: 13 g   Fiber: 3 g   Sugars: 10 g   Protein: 23 g

MACARONI AND CHEESE WITH BROCCOLI AND CHICKEN

SERVES: 8 (1½ cups each)   Prep Time: 20 min.   Cooking Time: 17 min.

CONTAINER EQUIVALENTS (per serving): ■ 1   ■ 1   ■ ½   ■ ½

4 oz.	**dry whole wheat macaroni (or 3 cups cooked macaroni)**
4 tsp.	**organic grass-fed butter (or organic coconut oil)**
2 Tbsp.	**unbleached whole wheat flour**
1½ cups	**unsweetened almond milk**
1¼ cups	**freshly grated extra-sharp cheddar cheese**
3 cups	**cooked chopped chicken breast, boneless, skinless**
6 cups	**chopped broccoli florets, steamed**
1 tsp.	**sea salt (or Himalayan salt)**
½ tsp.	**ground black pepper**

1. Cook macaroni according to package directions. (Do not use salt or oil if suggested in directions.) Set aside.

2. Melt butter in large saucepan over medium heat.

3. Add flour; cook, whisking constantly, for 1 minute, or until brown (don't let it burn).

4. Slowly whisk in almond milk; cook, whisking constantly, for 1 to 2 minutes, or until mixture thickens and there are no lumps.

5. Reduce heat to low. Add cheese; cook, whisking constantly, for 2 to 3 minutes, or until melted.

6. Add chicken, broccoli, salt, and pepper; cook, stirring constantly, for 1 minute, or until heated through.

7. Serve immediately.

TIP:

Use quinoa pasta and gluten-free flour if you're following a gluten-free lifestyle.

VARIATIONS:

- Asparagus, green beans, or brussels sprouts can be substituted for broccoli.

- A combination of cheeses like cheddar and Gouda, cheddar and Monterey jack, and cheddar and Asiago can be substituted for sharp cheddar.

NUTRITIONAL INFORMATION (per serving): Calories: 250
Total Fat: 10 g   Saturated Fat: 5 g   Cholesterol: 68 mg   Sodium: 491 mg   Carbohydrates: 15 g   Fiber: 2 g   Sugars: 0 g   Protein: 26 g

MEXICAN TACO MEAT

SERVES: 4 (approx. 1 cup each)   Prep Time: 20 min.   Cooking Time: 26 min.

CONTAINER EQUIVALENTS (per serving): ▌ ½   ▌ 1   ●— 1

1 tsp.	**olive oil**
1	**medium onion, chopped**
1	**medium jalapeño pepper, seeded, finely chopped**
2 cloves	**garlic, chopped**
1 lb.	**raw ground 93% lean turkey breast**
1 tsp.	**ground chili powder**
1 tsp.	**dried Mexican oregano leaves**
½ tsp.	**sea salt (or Himalayan salt)**
1 cup	**all-natural tomato sauce, no salt or sugar added**
1	**chipotle chile pepper in adobo sauce, chopped**
1 Tbsp.	**adobo sauce (the sauce from chipotle chile pepper in adobo sauce)**

1. Heat oil in large skillet over medium heat.
2. Add onion and jalapeno; cook, stirring frequently, for 4 to 5 minutes, or until onion is translucent.
3. Add garlic; cook, stirring frequently, for 1 minute. Transfer onion mixture to a medium bowl; set aside.
4. Add turkey to the same skillet; cook, over medium heat, stirring frequently to break up the turkey, for 8 to 10 minutes, or until the turkey is no longer pink.
5. Season with chili powder, oregano, and salt.
6. Add onion mixture, tomato sauce, chipotle chile pepper, and adobo sauce. Mix well. Reduce heat to medium-low; gently boil, stirring frequently, for 8 to 10 minutes, or until thickened.

SERVING SUGGESTIONS:
For one serving of Mexican Taco Meat

- Serve Mexican Taco Meat with 2 corn tortillas, 1 cup shredded lettuce, and 2 Tbsp. Homemade Salsa (recipe, pg. 85)
CONTAINER EQUIVALENTS (per serving): ▌ 1½   ▌ 1   ▌ 1   ●— 1

- Serve Mexican Taco Meat over 1 cup plain Zoodles (recipe, pg. 183) CONTAINER EQUIVALENTS (per serving): ▌ 1½   ▌ 1   ●— 1

- Serve Mexican Taco Meat over ½ cup cooked quinoa
CONTAINER EQUIVALENTS (per serving): ▌ 1½   ▌ 1   ▌ 1   ●— 1

- Serve Mexican Taco Meat inside 2 large romaine lettuce leaves
CONTAINER EQUIVALENTS (per serving): ▌ 1   ▌ 1   ●— 1

TIP:
Canned chipotle chile peppers in adobo sauce can be found in the Hispanic/Mexican aisle of many grocery stores. This product is generally gluten-free, however it would be wise to check the ingredients.

NUTRITIONAL INFORMATION Mexican Taco Meat only (per serving): Calories: 219
Total Fat: 11 g   Saturated Fat: 3 g   Cholesterol: 84 mg   Sodium: 477 mg   Carbohydrates: 9 g   Fiber: 3 g   Sugars: 4 g   Protein: 23 g

Recipes containing the **GF** icon are designed to be gluten-free, but please read product labels for each ingredient to ensure this to be the case.

PINEAPPLE CHICKEN SKEWERS

SERVES: 4 (2 skewers each)   Prep Time: 20 min.   Cooking Time: 10 min.

CONTAINER EQUIVALENTS (per serving): ▮ ½ ▮ ½ ▮ 1 ●— ½

8	**bamboo skewers**
1 lb.	**raw chicken breast, boneless, skinless, cut into 16 1-inch pieces**
¼ cup	**reduced-sodium tamari soy sauce, gluten-free**
2 tsp.	**sesame oil**
2 tsp.	**grated fresh ginger**
1 (8-oz.) can	**pineapple chunks in juice, drained**
1	**medium red bell pepper, cut into 16 1-inch chunks**
½	**large red onion, cut into 16 1-inch chunks**

1. Soak bamboo skewers in water for 30 minutes.

2. Place chicken in resealable plastic bag (or container); add soy sauce, oil, and ginger; seal bag and shake gently to mix. Refrigerate at least 30 minutes to marinate.

3. Preheat gas or charcoal grill on medium heat.

4. Place a piece of chicken, pineapple chunk, bell pepper, and onion onto a skewer. Repeat, so the skewer has two pieces of each ingredient. Repeat with seven remaining skewers. Discard marinade that contained chicken.

5. Grill skewers on covered grill for 4 to 5 minutes on each side, or until chicken is no longer pink in the middle.

6. Serve immediately.

TIP:

Leftover Pineapple Chicken Skewers can be used for lunch in the On-The-Go Salad (recipe, pg. 61).

NUTRITIONAL INFORMATION (per serving): Calories: 207
Total Fat: 5 g   Saturated Fat: 1 g   Cholesterol: 73 mg   Sodium: 594 mg   Carbohydrates: 12 g   Fiber: 1 g   Sugars: 9 g   Protein: 25 g

Recipes containing the GF icon are designed to be gluten-free, but please read product labels for each ingredient to ensure this to be the case.

BAKED TROUT

SERVES: 2   Prep Time: 15 min.   Cooking Time: 15 min.

CONTAINER EQUIVALENTS (per serving):   ■1   ■1   ■½   ●—½

1 (12-oz.)	raw, cleaned, cut open lengthwise, wild-caught trout
	Sea salt (or Himalayan salt) and ground black pepper (to taste; optional)
1	medium tomato, chopped
½	medium onion, chopped
1 clove	garlic, finely chopped
6	fresh basil leaves, finely chopped
1 tsp.	olive oil
1	medium lemon, sliced

1. Preheat oven to 425° F.
2. Season inside of trout with salt and pepper (if desired). Set aside.
3. Combine tomato, onion, garlic, and basil in a medium bowl; mix well.
4. Place trout on a large piece of aluminum foil (or parchment paper).
5. Fill inside of trout with tomato mixture.
6. Drizzle with oil and top with lemon slices; seal foil tightly. Place on a baking sheet. Bake for 10 to 12 minutes, or until trout is almost cooked through.
7. Increase oven temperature to broil.
8. Open foil to expose trout; broil for 2 to 3 minutes, or until skin is crisp and brown and trout flakes easily when tested with a fork.
9. Discard lemon slices. Evenly divide trout between two serving plates.

TIP:

To check if your fish is done, feel the meat along the spine; if it feels firm when you press on it, it's cooked through. You can also look inside the fish to see if all the pink flesh along the spine has turned white. If you see albumin (a thick white liquid) oozing from the flesh, your fish is overcooked.

RECIPE NOTE:

The half blue portion is there to account for the trout skin— a great source of heart-healthy omega-3 fatty acids. If you don't eat the skin, you can skip it.

NUTRITIONAL INFORMATION (per serving): Calories: 256
Total Fat: 8 g   Saturated Fat: 2 g   Cholesterol: 100 mg   Sodium: 200 mg   Carbohydrates: 8 g   Fiber: 2 g   Sugars: 4 g   Protein: 36 g

Recipes containing the GF icon are designed to be gluten-free, but please read product labels for each ingredient to ensure this to be the case.

SEARED AHI TUNA WITH PUMPKIN SEED SAUCE AND VEGGIES

SERVES: 4   Prep Time: 20 min.   Cooking Time: 17 min.

CONTAINER EQUIVALENTS (per serving): ■ 1 ■ 1 ■ ½

1 tsp.	olive oil
1	medium onion, cut into wedges
1	medium green bell pepper, sliced
1	medium red bell pepper, sliced
1 cup	halved cherry tomatoes
¼ tsp.	sea salt (or Himalayan salt)
¼ tsp.	ground black pepper
¼ tsp.	ground chili powder
4 (4-oz.)	raw ahi tuna steaks
4 Tbsp.	Pumpkin Seed Sauce (recipe, pg. 91)
4	large romaine lettuce leaves

1. Heat oil in a large nonstick skillet over medium heat.
2. Add onion and bell peppers; cook, stirring frequently, for 5 to 6 minutes, or until onion is translucent.
3. Add tomatoes; cook, stirring occasionally, for 2 to 3 minutes, or until tomatoes are soft. Remove vegetables from skillet. Set aside.
4. Combine salt, pepper, and chili powder in a small bowl; mix well.
5. Coat all sides of ahi steaks with seasoning.
6. Heat the same skillet over medium-high heat.
7. Add ahi; sear for 2 minutes on each side, or until desired doneness. Remove from heat.
8. Slice tuna on an angle.
9. Evenly spread Pumpkin Seed Sauce on four serving plates. Top evenly with ahi, a lettuce leaf, and vegetable mixture; serve immediately.

TIP:

Leftover cooked Seared Ahi Tuna can be used for lunch in the Seared Ahi Tuna Rice Bowl (recipe, pg. 137).

NUTRITIONAL INFORMATION (per serving): Calories: 217
Total Fat: 6 g   Saturated Fat: 0 g   Cholesterol: 44 mg   Sodium: 286 mg   Carbohydrates: 10 g   Fiber: 3 g   Sugars: 5 g   Protein: 31 g

Recipes containing the **GF** icon are designed to be gluten-free, but please read product labels for each ingredient to ensure this to be the case.

STEAK FAJITAS

SERVES: 4 (2 fajitas each)   Prep Time: 20 min.   Cooking Time: 18 min.

CONTAINER EQUIVALENTS (per serving): ■ 1   ▫ 1   ■ 1   ▬ 1

1½ tsp.	**olive oil**
2	**medium green (or red or yellow) bell peppers, cut into strips**
1	**medium onion, sliced**
2 cloves	**garlic, finely chopped**
1 lb.	**raw extra-lean beef sirloin, cut into 2-inch strips**
1 tsp.	**ground chili powder**
1 tsp.	**ground cumin**
1 tsp.	**crushed red pepper flakes**
½ tsp.	**sea salt (or Himalayan salt)**
½ cup	**Homemade Salsa (recipe, pg. 85)**
8	**6-inch corn tortillas, warm**
4 Tbsp.	**reduced fat (2%) plain Greek yogurt**
¼ cup	**chopped fresh cilantro**
	Lime wedges

1. Heat oil in large nonstick skillet over medium-high heat.

2. Add bell peppers and onion; cook, stirring occasionally, for 5 to 6 minutes, or until onion is translucent and peppers are tender.

3. Add garlic; cook, stirring frequently, for 1 minute.

4. Add beef, chili powder, cumin, pepper flakes, and salt; cook, stirring occasionally, for 7 to 8 minutes, or until meat is no longer pink.

5. Add salsa; cook, stirring frequently, for 2 to 3 minutes, or until heated through.

6. Evenly top each tortilla with beef mixture, yogurt, cilantro, and a squeeze of lime juice.

TIPS:

- Green, red, or yellow bell peppers, or a combination, can be used to make the fajitas.

- Leftover Steak Fajitas can be used for lunch in the Steak Salad (recipe, pg. 67).

NUTRITIONAL INFORMATION (per serving): Calories: 311
Total Fat: 8 g   Saturated Fat: 3 g   Cholesterol: 59 mg   Sodium: 430 mg   Carbohydrates: 30 g   Fiber: 5 g   Sugars: 4 g   Protein: 30 g

Recipes containing the **GF** icon are designed to be gluten-free, but please read product labels for each ingredient to ensure this to be the case.

SWEET POTATO RICOTTA GNUDI IN PUMPKIN SAUCE

SERVES: 3 (approx. 6 Gnudi each)   Prep Time: 30 min.   Cooking Time: 40 min.

CONTAINER EQUIVALENTS (per serving): ⬜ 2 ⬜ 1 ⬛ ½

PUMPKIN SAUCE:

1 tsp.	olive oil
¼ cup	chopped onion (⅓ medium onion)
2 cloves	garlic, finely chopped
1 cup	canned pumpkin puree
¼ cup	unsweetened almond milk
¼ tsp.	ground cinnamon
¼ tsp.	ground nutmeg
¼ tsp.	ground ginger
¼ tsp.	ground cloves

GNUDI:

4 cups	hot water
4	small sweet potatoes, peeled, cut into 1-inch cubes
1 Tbsp.	part-skim ricotta cheese
1	large egg yolk
1 pinch	sea salt (or Himalayan salt)
¼ tsp.	ground black pepper
	Coconut flour
1 tsp.	olive oil
4	fresh sage leaves
1 pinch	ground cinnamon (for garnish)
1 pinch	ground nutmeg (for garnish)
½ tsp.	raw honey

PUMPKIN SAUCE:

1. Heat oil in medium skillet over medium-high heat.
2. Add onion; cook, stirring frequently, for 3 to 5 minutes, or until onion is translucent.
3. Add garlic; cook, stirring frequently, for 1 minute.
4. Add pumpkin, almond milk, cinnamon, nutmeg, ginger, and cloves; cook, stirring frequently, for 4 to 5 minutes, or until sauce begins to boil. Remove from heat.
5. Place sauce in blender or food processor, in two or more batches, if necessary; cover with lid and kitchen towel. Blend until smooth.
6. Return sauce to skillet. Heat over medium heat, stirring frequently, for 1 to 2 minutes just before serving.

GNUDI:

1. Bring water to a boil in a large saucepan over medium-high heat.
2. Add sweet potatoes. Bring back to a boil. Reduce heat to low; gently boil for 15 to 20 minutes, or until sweet potatoes are fork tender. Remove from heat, drain, and place in an ice bath to cool.
3. When sweet potatoes are cool, drain, and mash until smooth.
4. Combine sweet potatoes, ricotta, egg yolk, salt, and pepper in a large bowl; mix well. Paste should be smooth, thick, and sticky to the touch.
5. Roll teaspoon-sized dollops between clean palms to form approximately eighteen oval dumplings.
6. Roll each dumpling in coconut flour to coat. If dumplings are very soft, refrigerate, covered, for 30 to 60 minutes. Set aside.
7. Heat oil in large skillet over medium-high heat.
8. Add sage; cook for 4 minutes, turning once. Remove crisp sage from oil. Place on a paper towel.
9. Add dumplings to oil; cook for 3 minutes, gently turning once, until light brown.
10. Evenly top each of three serving plates with pumpkin sauce, gnudi, cinnamon, nutmeg, and a drizzle of honey. Garnish with sage (if desired).

NUTRITIONAL INFORMATION (per serving): Calories: 267
Total Fat: 6 g   Saturated Fat: 2 g   Cholesterol: 63 mg   Sodium: 191 mg   Carbohydrates: 48 g   Fiber: 11 g   Sugars: 12 g   Protein: 7 g

Recipes containing the GF icon are designed to be gluten-free, but please read product labels for each ingredient to ensure this to be the case.

TURKEY CHILI

GF

SERVES: 8 (approx. 1½ cups each)   Prep Time: 20 min.   Cooking Time: 30 min.

CONTAINER EQUIVALENTS (per serving): ■ ½   ▫ 1   ■ 1   ●—½

2 tsp.	extra-virgin organic coconut oil, melted
1	medium onion, chopped
1	medium green bell pepper, chopped
1	medium red bell pepper, chopped
2 cloves	garlic, finely chopped
1 lb.	cooked 93% lean ground turkey breast (or lean grass-fed ground beef)
2 cans (15-oz. ea.)	kidney beans (or pinto beans), drained, rinsed
1 (15-oz.) can	organic diced tomatoes, no salt added
1 cup	red wine
1 Tbsp.	ground chili powder
½ tsp.	sea salt (or Himalayan salt)
2 tsp.	crushed red pepper (optional)
¼ cup	chopped fresh cilantro
8 tsp.	crumbled goat cheese

1. Heat oil in large saucepan over medium-high heat.
2. Add onion and bell peppers; cook, stirring occasionally, for 5 to 6 minutes, or until onion is translucent.
3. Add garlic; cook, stirring frequently, for 1 minute.
4. Add turkey, beans, tomatoes (with liquid), wine, chili powder, salt, and red pepper (if desired). Bring to a boil. Reduce heat; gently boil, stirring occasionally, for 20 minutes, or until slightly thickened.
5. Evenly divide between eight serving bowls; top with cilantro and cheese.

TIP:

This is an ideal recipe post-Thanksgiving, but it can be made all year round using ground turkey.

NUTRITIONAL INFORMATION (per serving): Calories: 288
Total Fat: 10 g   Saturated Fat: 4 g   Cholesterol: 61 mg   Sodium: 394 mg   Carbohydrates: 23 g   Fiber: 8 g   Sugars: 3 g   Protein: 23 g

Recipes containing the GF icon are designed to be gluten-free, but please read product labels for each ingredient to ensure this to be the case.

TURKEY SLOPPY JOES

SERVES: 4 (approx. 1 cup each)   Prep Time: 15 min.   Cooking Time: 36 min.

CONTAINER EQUIVALENTS (per serving): ■1 ■1 ●—1

1 tsp.	olive oil
1	medium onion, chopped
1	medium red bell pepper, chopped
2 cloves	garlic, chopped
1 lb.	raw ground 93% lean turkey breast
½ tsp.	sea salt (or Himalayan salt)
¼ tsp.	ground black pepper
1 cup	all-natural tomato sauce, no salt or sugar added
1 Tbsp.	Worcestershire sauce, gluten-free
1½ tsp.	hot pepper sauce
1 Tbsp.	pure maple syrup (or raw honey)
	Finely chopped fresh parsley (optional)

1. Heat oil in large skillet over medium heat.
2. Add onion and bell pepper; cook, stirring frequently, for 4 to 5 minutes, or until onion is translucent.
3. Add garlic; cook, stirring frequently, for 1 minute. Transfer onion mixture to a medium bowl. Set aside.
4. Add turkey to the same skillet; cook, over medium heat, stirring frequently to break up the turkey, for 8 to 10 minutes, or until the turkey is no longer pink.
5. Season with salt and pepper.
6. Add onion mixture, tomato sauce, Worcestershire sauce, pepper sauce, and maple syrup. Mix well. Reduce heat to medium-low; gently boil, stirring occasionally, for 15 to 20 minutes, or until sauce has thickened.
7. Sprinkle each serving with parsley before serving (if desired).

SERVING SUGGESTIONS:
For one serving of Turkey Sloppy Joes

- Serve Turkey Sloppy Joes open-faced on one slice of low-sodium whole-grain sprouted bread
  CONTAINER EQUIVALENTS (per serving): ■1 □1 ■1 ●—1
- Serve Turkey Sloppy Joes over 1 cup plain Zoodles (recipe, pg. 183)
  CONTAINER EQUIVALENTS (per serving): ■2 ■1 ●—1
- Serve Turkey Sloppy Joes over ½ cup cooked whole wheat (or quinoa) pasta
  CONTAINER EQUIVALENTS (per serving): ■1 □1 ■1 ●—1
- Serve Sloppy Joes in 2 large romaine lettuce leaves
  CONTAINER EQUIVALENTS (per serving): ■1½ ■1 ●—1

NUTRITIONAL INFORMATION Turkey Sloppy Joes only (per serving): Calories: 238
Total Fat: 11 g   Saturated Fat: 3 g   Cholesterol: 84 mg   Sodium: 426 mg   Carbohydrates: 13 g   Fiber: 2 g   Sugars: 9 g   Protein: 23 g

Recipes containing the GF icon are designed to be gluten-free, but please read product labels for each ingredient to ensure this to be the case.

SIDES

CUCUMBER HUMMUS ROLL-UPS

SERVES: 2 (4 roll-ups each)   Prep Time: 15 min.   Cooking Time: None

CONTAINER EQUIVALENTS (per serving): ■ ½   ■ ½

1	**large cucumber**
¼ cup	**store-bought hummus**
¼ cup	**roasted red bell peppers, thinly sliced**
	Toothpicks

1. Use a vegetable peeler to peel off long, thin slices of cucumber.
2. Spread hummus evenly on each cucumber slice.
3. Top evenly with roasted pepper slices.
4. Pick up one end of the cucumber slice and roll cucumber loosely around the filling. End with the seam on bottom and secure with a toothpick.

VARIATIONS:
(substitute for roasted red bell peppers)

- Chopped fresh red bell peppers
- Sun-dried tomatoes
- Capers
- Fresh chopped herbs
- Sliced green onions

NUTRITIONAL INFORMATION (per serving): Calories: 72
Total Fat: 3 g Saturated Fat: 0 g Cholesterol: 0 mg Sodium: 142 mg Carbohydrates: 8 g Fiber: 3 g Sugars: 2 g Protein: 3 g

Recipes containing the **GF** icon are designed to be gluten-free, but please read product labels for each ingredient to ensure this to be the case.

POTATO SIDES

SERVES: 4 (¾ cup each) Prep Time: 15 min. Cooking Time: 20 min.

CONTAINER EQUIVALENTS (per serving): 1½ ●—1

4	**medium sweet potatoes (or Yukon gold potatoes), cut into 1-inch cubes**
1	**large onion, cut into 1-inch pieces (optional)**
4 tsp.	**olive oil**
½ tsp.	**sea salt (or Himalayan salt)**
½ tsp.	**ground black pepper**

1. Preheat oven to 450° F.
2. Place sweet potatoes and onion (if desired) on baking sheet.
3. Drizzle with oil; toss gently to coat evenly.
   Spread sweet potato mixture out in a single layer.
4. Bake, stirring halfway, for 18 to 22 minutes, or until tender.
5. Season with salt and pepper; serve immediately.

SUGGESTED ADDITIONS:

- Chopped fresh rosemary and fresh garlic
- Chopped fresh flat leaf (Italian) parsley and crushed red pepper
- Ground chili powder and chopped fresh garlic
- Dried thyme and marjoram leaves

NUTRITIONAL INFORMATION (per serving): Calories: 167
Total Fat: 5 g Saturated Fat: 1 g Cholesterol: 0 mg Sodium: 358 mg Carbohydrates: 30 g Fiber: 5 g Sugars: 7 g Protein: 3 g

Recipes containing the GF icon are designed to be gluten-free, but please read product labels for each ingredient to ensure this to be the case.

ROASTED ACORN SQUASH

SERVES: 4 (½ squash each)   Prep Time: 10 min.   Cooking Time: 55 min.

CONTAINER EQUIVALENTS (per serving):   ▮ 2   ●—1

	Nonstick cooking spray
2	small acorn squash, halved, seeded
½ tsp.	sea salt (or Himalayan salt)
½ tsp.	ground black pepper
4 tsp.	unsalted organic grass-fed butter
4 tsp.	pure maple syrup
1 tsp.	ground cinnamon
½ tsp.	ground nutmeg

1. Preheat oven to 350° F.
2. Coat large baking sheet with spray.
   Place squash, cut side down, on baking sheet.
3. Bake for 30 to 35 minutes, or until tender-crisp.
4. Turn cut side up. Season with salt and pepper.
   Dot each half with 1 tsp. butter; drizzle with 1 tsp. maple syrup.
   Sprinkle evenly with cinnamon and nutmeg.
5. Bake for 15 to 20 additional minutes, or until tender.

NUTRITIONAL INFORMATION (per serving): Calories: 123
Total Fat: 4 g   Saturated Fat: 2 g   Cholesterol: 10 mg   Sodium: 304 mg   Carbohydrates: 22 g   Fiber: 3 g   Sugars: 4 g   Protein: 1 g

Recipes containing the (GF) icon are designed to be gluten-free, but please read product labels for each ingredient to ensure this to be the case.

SPICY CAULIFLOWER BITES

SERVES: 5 (1 cup each)   Prep Time: 20 min.   Cooking Time: 35 min.

CONTAINER EQUIVALENTS (per serving):   ■ 2   ■ ½   ▬ 1

I always try to bring a somewhat healthy dish to parties, but I don't want to be that person who always brings the vegetable platter. This is a great way to bring something interesting that can be passed off as not-so-healthy. (Shhh...)

	Nonstick cooking spray
6 cups	cauliflower florets
½ tsp.	sea salt (or Himalayan salt), *divided use*
½ cup	hot pepper sauce
⅓ cup	rice vinegar
1 Tbsp.	cornstarch, gluten-free (preferably GMO-free)
2 tsp.	ground chili powder
¼ tsp.	ground smoked paprika
½ tsp.	garlic powder
½ tsp.	onion powder
1 tsp.	pure maple syrup
1 tsp.	Worcestershire sauce, gluten-free
2 Tbsp.	organic grass-fed butter
3 cups	celery sticks
6 Tbsp.	Lemon Garlic Sauce (recipe, pg. 87)

1. Preheat oven to 350° F.
2. Lightly coat large baking sheet with spray.
3. Place cauliflower florets on baking sheet. Coat cauliflower lightly with spray. Season evenly with ¼ tsp. salt.
4. Bake for 20 minutes, or until tender-crisp.
5. While cauliflower is baking, combine hot sauce, vinegar, and cornstarch in medium saucepan; whisk until cornstarch is dissolved.
6. Add chili powder, paprika, garlic powder, onion powder, maple syrup, Worcestershire sauce, butter, and *remaining ¼ tsp.* salt; whisk to blend.
7. Heat hot sauce mixture over medium-high heat; cook, stirring frequently, for 10 minutes, or until thickened. Set aside.
8. Pour hot sauce mixture over baked cauliflower (on baking sheet); mix well.
9. Return cauliflower to oven. Bake for 5 minutes.
10. Serve hot with celery sticks and Lemon Garlic Sauce.

NUTRITIONAL INFORMATION (per serving): Calories: 159
Total Fat: 11 g   Saturated Fat: 4 g   Cholesterol: 34 mg   Sodium: 598 mg   Carbohydrates: 14 g   Fiber: 3 g   Sugars: 6 g   Protein: 3 g

Recipes containing the **GF** icon are designed to be gluten-free, but please read product labels for each ingredient to ensure this to be the case.

ZOODLES (ZUCCHINI PASTA)

GF VG

SERVES: 4 (1 cup each)   Prep Time: 15 min.   Cooking Time: 3 min.

CONTAINER EQUIVALENTS (per serving): ▢ 1½   ▢ ½

4	**medium zucchini**
	Hot water
1 cup	**Grandma's Tomato Sauce (recipe, pg. 81), warm**
2 Tbsp.	**finely shredded fresh basil**
2 Tbsp.	**grated Parmesan cheese**

1. Using a vegetable peeler, cut each zucchini into lengthwise strips about ⅛-inch thick. Turn zucchini slightly after cutting each strip to work evenly around the outside, stopping when you hit the seeds at the core. Discard cores. Cut slices lengthwise into ½-inch ribbons. Set aside.

2. Boil water in steamer (or large saucepan) over high heat. Reduce heat to medium-high. Place zucchini in steamer basket; cook for 2 to 3 minutes, or until tender. Remove from heat.

3. Divide zucchini evenly between four serving plates; top evenly with Grandma's Tomato Sauce, basil, and cheese.

TIP:

Zucchini can also be sliced on a mandoline; adjust to a very thin slice.

VARIATION:
(substitute spaghetti squash for Zoodles)

Place a medium **spaghetti squash** (about 3 lbs.) on a parchment-lined baking sheet. Poke the squash 2 or 3 times with a fork. Bake at 350° F. for 60 to 80 minutes. Cool for 20 to 30 minutes. Cut squash in half lengthwise. Remove seeds. Scrape flesh into stringy noodles. Serve four portions topped with Grandma's Tomato Sauce, basil, and cheese.

NUTRITIONAL INFORMATION (per serving): Calories: 109
Total Fat: 4 g   Saturated Fat: 1 g   Cholesterol: 5 mg   Sodium: 235 mg   Carbohydrates: 13 g   Fiber: 4 g   Sugars: 10 g   Protein: 6 g

Recipes containing the GF icon are designed to be gluten-free, but please read product labels for each ingredient to ensure this to be the case.

ZUCCHINI BAKE

GF VG

SERVES: 4 (approx. 4 spears each)   Prep Time: 15 min.   Cooking Time: 20 min.

CONTAINER EQUIVALENTS (per serving): ■ 2   ■ ½   ●— 1

½ cup	**grated Parmesan cheese**
2 Tbsp.	**freshly grated lemon peel**
½ tsp.	**dried thyme leaves**
½ tsp.	**dried oregano leaves**
½ tsp.	**sea salt (or Himalayan salt)**
½ tsp.	**ground black pepper**
2 cloves	**garlic, finely chopped**
4	**large zucchini, quartered lengthwise**
1 Tbsp.	**olive oil**
	Lemon wedges

1. Preheat oven to 350° F.

2. Combine cheese, lemon peel, thyme, oregano, salt, pepper, and garlic in a small bowl; mix well. Set aside.

3. Place zucchini skin side down in large baking dish. Brush with oil, covering all of zucchini. Sprinkle evenly with cheese mixture.

4. Bake for 15 to 20 minutes, or until tender.

5. Serve with lemon wedges.

NUTRITIONAL INFORMATION (per serving): Calories: 146
Total Fat: 8 g   Saturated Fat: 3 g   Cholesterol: 11 mg   Sodium: 503 mg   Carbohydrates: 12 g   Fiber: 4 g   Sugars: 9 g   Protein: 9 g

Recipes containing the GF icon are designed to be gluten-free, but please read product labels for each ingredient to ensure this to be the case.

ALMOND CHOCOLATE PROTEIN SQUARES

SERVES: 16 (1 square each)   Prep Time: 15 min.   Cooking Time: None

CONTAINER EQUIVALENTS (per serving):   ½   ½   2

1 cup	**oat flour, gluten-free**
1 cup	**whey protein powder, vanilla flavor**
½ cup	**almond flour**
½ tsp.	**sea salt (or Himalayan salt)**
1 cup	**all-natural almond butter**
2 tsp.	**pure vanilla extract**
½ cup	**unsweetened almond milk**
¼ cup	**dark chocolate chips, melted according to package directions**

1. Line 8 x 8-inch baking pan with parchment paper. Set aside.
2. Place oat flour, protein powder, almond flour, and salt in food processor; pulse to mix.
3. Add almond butter and extract; pulse for 1 minute, or until crumbly.
4. Add almond milk; pulse for 1 minute, or until mixture forms a soft dough.
5. Press dough into prepared pan. Smooth top with a spatula.
6. Freeze, covered, for 15 minutes.
7. Cut into sixteen squares (2 x 2-inches each).
8. Drizzle melted chocolate evenly on top of protein squares.
9. Freeze for 10 minutes, or until chocolate sets.
10. Store in freezer for up to one week in airtight container.

VARIATIONS:

- You can substitute almond butter with peanut butter, cashew butter, seed butters, or hazelnut butter.
- Almond flour can be substituted with coconut flour or hazelnut flour.

TIPS:

- If you want to make sure these protein squares are gluten-free, look for certified gluten-free oats or oat flour. Oats are a naturally gluten-free food, however they are easily contaminated with gluten during harvesting. Therefore, to ensure you have a gluten-free product, look for the gluten-free variety.
- You can make your own oat flour by processing oats in a food processor or blender until smooth.
- You can make your own almond flour by processing 1 cup slivered almonds in a food processor (or blender with a strong motor). Make sure that you pulse in 20-second intervals to prevent the almonds from turning into almond butter. 1 cup of slivered almonds yields approximately 1 cup of almond flour.
- If you can't find almond flour in your store, you can look at club stores or online.

NUTRITIONAL INFORMATION (per serving): Calories: 182
Total Fat: 13 g   Saturated Fat: 2 g   Cholesterol: 7 mg   Sodium: 122 mg   Carbohydrates: 11 g   Fiber: 3 g   Sugars: 3 g   Protein: 8 g

AUTUMN'S BANANA APPLE MUFFINS

SERVES: 9 (1 muffin each)   Prep Time: 20 min.   Cooking Time: 18 min.

CONTAINER EQUIVALENTS (per serving): ■ 1 ■ 1

My son is a big eater, except first thing in the morning, so this recipe started out as a way of tricking him into eating something deceptively healthy when he wakes up. But now everybody loves these super "healthified" muffins because they're delicious and taste just like a regular old not-so-great-for-you muffin.

2	large eggs, lightly beaten
1 cup	mashed ripe banana (about 2 medium bananas)
1 Tbsp.	organic grass-fed butter, melted
1½ cups	almond flour
¾ tsp.	baking soda, gluten-free
1 dash	sea salt (or Himalayan salt)
½ cup	chopped apple (about ¾ medium apple)

1. Preheat oven to 350° F.
2. Prepare nine muffin cups by lining with muffin tin liners or coating with spray.
3. Combine eggs, banana, and butter in a medium bowl; mix well. Set aside.
4. Combine almond flour, baking soda, and salt in a medium bowl; mix well.
5. Add almond meal mixture to egg mixture; mix until blended.
6. Add apple; mix until just blended.
7. Divide batter evenly between prepared muffin cups.
8. Bake 18 to 22 minutes, or until golden brown and toothpick inserted into the center comes out clean.
9. Transfer muffins to rack; cool.

TIPS:

- If you'd like a little more fiber and some omega-3 fatty acids, replace ½ cup of your almond flour with ½ cup of flaxseed meal.
- You can make your own almond flour by processing 1 cup slivered almonds in a food processor (or blender with a strong motor) Make sure that you pulse in 20-second intervals to prevent the almonds from turning into almond butter. 1 cup of slivered almonds yields approximately 1 cup of almond flour.
- If you can't find almond flour in your store, you can look at club stores or online.

NUTRITIONAL INFORMATION (per serving): Calories: 161
Total Fat: 12 g   Saturated Fat: 2 g   Cholesterol: 45 mg   Sodium: 157 mg   Carbohydrates: 11 g   Fiber: 3 g   Sugars: 4 g   Protein: 6 g

Recipes containing the **GF** icon are designed to be gluten-free, but please read product labels for each ingredient to ensure this to be the case.

HOMEMADE GRANOLA

SERVES: 30 (2 Tbsp. each)   Prep Time: 15 min.   Cooking Time: 45 min.

CONTAINER EQUIVALENTS (per serving): ½ ½ 1

2½ cups	**quinoa flakes (or gluten-free old-fashioned rolled oats)**
½ cup	**sliced raw almonds**
½ cup	**chopped raw walnuts**
½ cup	**shredded unsweetened dried coconut**
¼ cup	**chopped dried apricots**
¼ cup	**unsweetened dried cranberries**
1½ tsp.	**ground cinnamon**
¼ tsp.	**sea salt (or Himalayan salt)**
¼ cup	**pure maple syrup**
3 Tbsp.	**extra-virgin organic coconut oil**
½ cup	**unsweetened applesauce**

1. Preheat oven to 300° F.
2. Line baking sheet with parchment paper. Set aside.
3. Combine quinoa flakes, almonds, walnuts, coconut, apricots, cranberries, cinnamon, and salt in a large mixing bowl; mix well. Set aside.
4. Heat maple syrup, oil, and applesauce in a small saucepan over low heat; cook, stirring constantly, for 4 to 5 minutes, or until oil has melted.
5. Pour maple syrup mixture over quinoa flake mixture; mix until flakes are evenly coated.
6. Place on prepared baking sheet; spread evenly in a thin layer.
7. Bake for 40 to 45 minutes, stirring every 15 minutes, or until granola is light golden brown and crisp.
8. Cool granola completely (it will get more crisp as it cools).
9. Store in an airtight container.

VARIATIONS:

Nuts or Seeds
(substitute ½ cup for walnuts or almonds):

- Cashews
- Toasted pecans
- Pine nuts
- Raw pumpkin seeds
- Raw sunflower seeds

Dried Fruit
(substitute ¼ cup for cranberries or apricots):

- Apples
- Blueberries
- Figs
- Mangoes
- Raisins
- Pears

SERVING SUGGESTION:

Serve ¾ cup reduced fat (2%) yogurt topped with 2 Tbsp. granola and ½ cup mixed berries.

CONTAINER EQUIVALENTS (per serving): ½ ½ 1 ½ 1

NUTRITIONAL INFORMATION Homemade Granola only (per serving): Calories: 133
Total Fat: 9 g   Saturated Fat: 6 g   Cholesterol: 0 mg   Sodium: 23 mg   Carbohydrates: 12 g   Fiber: 2 g   Sugars: 5 g   Protein: 2 g

Recipes containing the GF icon are designed to be gluten-free, but please read product labels for each ingredient to ensure this to be the case.

PUMPKIN MUFFINS WITH MAPLE CREAM CHEESE

SERVES: 9 (1 muffin each)   Prep Time: 15 min.   Cooking Time: 18 min.

CONTAINER EQUIVALENTS (per serving): ■ 1 ■ 1

2 oz.	**cream cheese**
1 Tbsp.	**pure maple syrup**
1	**large egg, lightly beaten**
1 cup	**canned pumpkin puree**
1½ cups	**almond flour**
¾ tsp.	**baking soda, gluten-free**
1 dash	**sea salt (or Himalayan salt)**
2 Tbsp.	**raw pumpkin seeds**

1. Preheat oven to 350° F.
2. Prepare nine muffin cups by lining with muffin tin liners or coating with spray. Set aside.
3. Combine cream cheese and maple syrup in a small bowl; mix well. Set aside.
4. Combine egg and pumpkin in a medium bowl; mix well. Set aside.
5. Combine almond flour, baking soda, and salt in a medium bowl; mix well.
6. Add almond meal mixture to egg mixture; mix until just blended.
7. Spoon batter into each prepared muffin cup, filling a little less than ½ full.
8. Spoon about 1 heaping tsp. cream cheese mixture into the center of each muffin. Evenly fill muffin cups ¾ full with remaining batter.
9. Sprinkle muffins evenly with pumpkin seeds.
10. Bake 18 to 22 minutes, or until golden brown and toothpick inserted into the center comes out clean.
11. Transfer muffins to rack; cool.

TIPS:

- You can make your own almond flour by processing 1 cup slivered almonds in a food processor (or blender with a strong motor). Make sure that you pulse in 20-second intervals to prevent the almonds from turning into almond butter. 1 cup of slivered almonds yields approximately 1 cup of almond flour.
- If you can't find almond flour in your store, you can look at club stores or online.

RECIPE NOTE:

While the pumpkin puree in these muffins earns them a purple container portion, nothing replaces fresh, whole fruit in a healthy diet, so I encourage you to limit muffin intake to one per day.

NUTRITIONAL INFORMATION (per serving): Calories: 161
Total Fat: 13 g   Saturated Fat: 2 g   Cholesterol: 28 mg   Sodium: 166 mg   Carbohydrates: 8 g   Fiber: 3 g   Sugars: 3 g   Protein: 6 g

Recipes containing the GF icon are designed to be gluten-free, but please read product labels for each ingredient to ensure this to be the case.

PUMPKIN PIE ENERGY BITES

SERVES: 8 (2 energy bites each)   Prep Time: 20 min.   Cooking Time: None

CONTAINER EQUIVALENTS (per serving): ■ 1   ■ ½

1 cup	**pitted dates**
	Warm water
½ cup	**raw pecan halves (or pecan pieces)**
⅓ cup	**canned pumpkin puree**
¼ cup	**unsweetened coconut flakes, reserve small amount for garnish**
1 tsp.	**pure hazelnut extract (or pure maple extract)**
1 tsp.	**pure maple syrup**
2 tsp.	**pumpkin pie spice**
1 pinch	**sea salt (or Himalayan salt)**

1. Place dates in a medium bowl; cover with water. Let soak for 10 minutes. Drain. Set aside.

2. Place pecans in food processor; pulse until finely ground.

3. Add dates, pumpkin, coconut, extract, maple syrup, pumpkin pie spice, and salt; pulse until well mixed. Place in a medium bowl. Refrigerate, covered, for 30 minutes.

4. Using clean hands, roll into tablespoon-sized balls; roll in reserved coconut (if desired).

5. Store, refrigerated, in airtight container.

6. Cool completely; divide evenly among 4 servings.

NUTRITIONAL INFORMATION (per serving): Calories: 122
Total Fat: 6 g Saturated Fat: 2 g Cholesterol: 0 mg Sodium: 20 mg Carbohydrates: 17 g Fiber: 3 g Sugars: 13 g Protein: 1 g

Recipes containing the **GF** icon are designed to be gluten-free, but please read product labels for each ingredient to ensure this to be the case.

SPICED NUTS

SERVES: 16 (2 Tbsp. each)   Prep Time: 10 min.   Cooking Time: 8 min.

CONTAINER EQUIVALENTS (per serving): ▪ 1

1 tsp.	**ground chili powder**
¼ tsp.	**ground cayenne pepper**
½ tsp.	**sea salt (or Himalayan salt)**
2 cups	**mixed raw nuts**
2 tsp.	**extra-virgin organic coconut oil (or olive oil)**

1. Line baking sheet with parchment paper; set aside.
2. Combine chili powder, cayenne pepper, and salt in a small bowl; mix well. Set aside.
3. Heat nuts in large skillet over medium heat; cook, stirring frequently, for 3 to 4 minutes, or until toasted.
4. Add oil; cook, stirring constantly, for 30 seconds.
5. Add spice mixture; cook, stirring constantly, for 1 minute, or until nuts are well coated.
6. Reduce heat to medium-low; cook, stirring frequently, for 2 minutes.
7. Transfer nuts to the prepared baking sheet. Allow nuts to cool completely before transferring them to an airtight container for storage.
8. Nuts can be stored in a dry, cool area for up to 3 weeks.

VARIATION:

Maple Cinnamon Nuts Substitute 1 tsp. ground cinnamon for chili powder and cayenne pepper. Eliminate oil. Follow steps 1 to 3 above. Add ⅓ cup pure maple syrup (or raw honey) to skillet; cook, stirring frequently, for 2 minutes. Transfer nuts to the prepared baking pan. Allow nuts to cool completely before transferring them to an airtight container for storage.

NUTRITIONAL INFORMATION (per serving): Calories: 103
Total Fat: 10 g   Saturated Fat: 1 g   Cholesterol: 0 mg   Sodium: 75 mg   Carbohydrates: 3 g   Fiber: 2 g   Sugars: 1 g   Protein: 3 g

Recipes containing the GF icon are designed to be gluten-free, but please read product labels for each ingredient to ensure this to be the case.

SWEET POTATO CHIPS

SERVES: 4   Prep Time: 10 min.   Cooking Time: 3 hrs.

CONTAINER EQUIVALENTS (per serving): ½   ●— ½

2	**medium sweet potatoes, peeled, very thinly sliced**
2 tsp.	**extra-virgin organic coconut oil (or olive oil), melted**
¼ tsp.	**sea salt (or Himalayan salt)**

1. Preheat oven to 200° F.
2. Line two large baking sheets with parchment paper.
3. Place sweet potatoes on baking sheets in a single layer.
4. Brush with oil; sprinkle with salt.
5. Bake for 2 to 3 hours, or until crisp.
6. Cool completely; divide evenly among 4 servings.

NUTRITIONAL INFORMATION (per serving): Calories: 76
Total Fat: 2 g   Saturated Fat: 2 g   Cholesterol: 0 mg   Sodium: 178 mg   Carbohydrates: 13 g   Fiber: 2 g   Sugars: 3 g   Protein: 1 g

ZUCCHINI CHIPS

SERVES: 4   Prep Time: 15 min.   Cooking Time: 2 hrs.

CONTAINER EQUIVALENTS (per serving): ■ 1   ●— ½

2	**large zucchini, very thinly sliced**
1 Tbsp.	**olive oil**
½ tsp.	**sea salt (or Himalayan salt)**

1. Preheat oven to 225° F.
2. Place zucchini slices in one layer between paper towels to help draw out liquid.
3. Line two large baking sheets with parchment paper.
4. Place zucchini slices on prepared baking sheets.
5. Brush zucchini with oil; sprinkle with salt.
6. Bake for 2 hours, or until golden brown and crispy.
7. Cool completely; divide evenly among 4 servings.

NUTRITIONAL INFORMATION (per serving): Calories: 57
Total Fat: 4 g   Saturated Fat: 1 g   Cholesterol: 0 mg   Sodium: 298 mg   Carbohydrates: 5 g   Fiber: 2 g   Sugars: 4 g   Protein: 2 g

Recipes containing the icon are designed to be gluten-free, but please read product labels for each ingredient to ensure this to be the case.

DESSERTS

ALMOND MILK PANNA COTTA WITH BLUEBERRY JAM AND ITALIAN MERINGUE

SERVES: 4 (approx. ½ cup each)   Prep Time: 15 min.   Cooking Time: 15 min.

CONTAINER EQUIVALENTS (per serving): 1

¼ cup + 2 Tbsp.	raw honey, *divided use*
2 Tbsp.	water
2	large egg whites (¼ cup)
1 Tbsp.	fresh lemon juice
¾ tsp.	pure vanilla extract, *divided use*
2 cups	unsweetened almond milk
2½ tsp.	unsweetened gelatin
4 Tbsp.	Blueberry Jam (recipe, pg. 77)

1. To make Italian Meringue, place ¼ *cup* honey and water in small saucepan; cook, over medium-high heat, stirring occasionally, until mixture reaches 240° F. with a candy thermometer.

2. While honey cooks, place egg whites and lemon juice in a clean, large metal mixing bowl; beat until soft peaks are formed. Set aside.

3. When the honey mixture reaches 240° F., transfer it into a clean, heat-resistant pouring vessel (like a Pyrex measuring cup).

4. Slowly add honey mixture (in a thin stream) to egg whites, whisking vigorously until completely mixed.

5. Add ½ *tsp.* extract; continue whisking vigorously until the meringue forms stiff, glossy peaks. Set aside 4 Tbsp. for topping Panna Cotta. Refrigerate the remainder for up to 4 days.

6. Combine almond milk, *remaining 2 Tbsp.* honey, and gelatin in medium saucepan; whisk to blend. Set aside for 5 minutes.

7. Heat almond milk mixture over medium-low heat, stirring frequently, for about 5 to 8 minutes, or until just before mixture starts to boil. Remove from heat.

8. Add *remaining ¼ tsp.* extract; mix well. Cool for 20 minutes.

9. Pour into four serving bowls (or wine glasses). Refrigerate for 6 hours, or until gelatin has set.

10. Top each Panna Cotta with 1 Tbsp. Blueberry Jam and 1 Tbsp. Italian Meringue; serve immediately.

TIPS:

- Italian Meringue makes a healthier substitution for whipped cream. You can eat the leftovers from this recipe over fresh fruit for a delicious dessert.

- If you have a stand mixer, this would be a good way to beat the egg whites. If you don't, you might have someone slowly pour the honey mixture while you beat the egg whites.

NUTRITIONAL INFORMATION (per serving): Calories: 107
Total Fat: 2 g   Saturated Fat: 0 g   Cholesterol: 0 mg   Sodium: 116 mg   Carbohydrates: 20 g   Fiber: 1 g   Sugars: 17 g   Protein: 5 g

Recipes containing the GF icon are designed to be gluten-free, but please read product labels for each ingredient to ensure this to be the case.

CHOCOLATE CHIA PUDDING WITH STRAWBERRIES

SERVES: 6 (¾ cup each)   Prep Time: 20 min.   Cooking Time: None

CONTAINER EQUIVALENTS (per serving): ⬜ 1 ⬛ ½ ⬛ ½

2½ cups	**unsweetened almond milk**
½ cup	**chia seeds**
6 Tbsp.	**organic unsweetened cocoa powder**
2 Tbsp.	**pure maple syrup**
2 tsp.	**pure vanilla extract**
¼ tsp.	**sea salt (or Himalayan salt)**
3 cups	**chopped strawberries**

1. Combine almond milk, chia seeds, cocoa powder, maple syrup, extract, and salt in a large bowl; whisk vigorously for 2 minutes, or until cocoa powder is incorporated, and pudding is well blended.

2. Let stand at room temperature for 30 minutes; mix well. Refrigerate, covered, for 4 hours or overnight, stirring occasionally.

3. Divide evenly into six small serving bowls; top each serving with ½ cup strawberries.

VARIATION:

This pudding could also be topped with chopped banana, fresh blueberries, fresh raspberries, chopped kiwifruit, or chopped pear.

NUTRITIONAL INFORMATION (per serving): Calories: 154
Total Fat: 6 g   Saturated Fat: 0 g   Cholesterol: 0 mg   Sodium: 174 mg   Carbohydrates: 21 g   Fiber: 8 g   Sugars: 8 g   Protein: 4 g

Recipes containing the **GF** icon are designed to be gluten-free, but please read product labels for each ingredient to ensure this to be the case.

CHOCOLATE CHIP COOKIES

SERVES: 26 (1 cookie each)   Prep Time: 20 min.   Cooking Time: 16 min.

CONTAINER EQUIVALENTS (per serving): ◻ 1½

3 cups	**almond flour**
1 tsp.	**baking soda, gluten-free**
¼ tsp.	**sea salt (or Himalayan salt)**
¼ cup	**extra-virgin organic coconut oil, melted**
¼ cup	**pure maple syrup (or raw honey)**
1	**large egg**
2	**large egg whites (¼ cup)**
1 tsp.	**pure vanilla extract**
½ cup	**semi-sweet (or dark) chocolate chips**

1. Preheat oven to 375° F.
2. Line two baking sheets with parchment paper. Set aside.
3. Combine almond flour, baking soda, and salt in a medium bowl; mix well. Set aside.
4. Beat oil and maple syrup in a large mixer bowl until creamy, approximately 4 to 5 minutes.
5. Add egg, egg whites, and extract; beat for an additional 2 minutes.
6. Add almond flour mixture to egg mixture; mix until blended.
7. Add chocolate chips; mix until just blended.
8. Drop by rounded Tbsp. onto prepared baking sheets. Flatten cookies with a spatula if traditional cookie appearance is desired. Bake for 14 to 16 minutes, or until golden brown.
9. Store in an airtight container.

TIPS:

- You can make your own almond flour by processing 1 cup slivered almonds in a food processor (or blender with a strong motor). Make sure that you pulse in 20-second intervals to prevent the almonds from turning into almond butter. 1 cup of slivered almonds yields approximately 1 cup of almond flour.

- If you can't find almond flour in your store, you can look at club stores or online.

NUTRITIONAL INFORMATION (per serving): Calories: 126
Total Fat: 10 g   Saturated Fat: 3 g   Cholesterol: 7 mg   Sodium: 78 mg   Carbohydrates: 8 g   Fiber: 2 g   Sugars: 5 g   Protein: 3 g

Recipes containing the GF icon are designed to be gluten-free, but please read product labels for each ingredient to ensure this to be the case.

CHUNKY MONKEY ICE CREAM

SERVES: 4 (approx. ¼ cup each)   Prep Time: 15 min.   Cooking Time: None

CONTAINER EQUIVALENTS (per serving):   ▮ 1   ●— 3½

I admit it. Sometimes I want ice cream, but I don't want all the empty calories from sugar. The frozen banana and the sliced almonds in Chunky Monkey give me tons of flavor (so I don't even miss the sugar) and it still feels like a treat.

3	**ripe medium bananas, cut into chunks**	1.	Place bananas in plastic bag; freeze for 4 hours, or until completely frozen.
3 Tbsp.	**all-natural peanut butter**	2.	Place bananas and peanut butter in blender (or food processor); cover. Blend until smooth. Add 1 to 2 Tbsp. almond milk, if needed, for creamier texture.
	Unsweetened almond milk (optional)		
4 tsp.	**chopped dark chocolate**	3.	Divide ice cream evenly between four serving bowls; top evenly with chocolate and almonds.
4 tsp.	**sliced raw almonds**	4.	Serve immediately.

NUTRITIONAL INFORMATION (per serving): Calories: 182

Total Fat: 9 g   Saturated Fat: 2 g   Cholesterol: 0 mg   Sodium: 57 mg   Carbohydrates: 25 g   Fiber: 4 g   Sugars: 13 g   Protein: 5 g

Recipes containing the GF icon are designed to be gluten-free, but please read product labels for each ingredient to ensure this to be the case.

FLOURLESS CHOCOLATE CHICKPEA BROWNIES

SERVES: 16 (1 brownie each)   Prep Time: 20 min.   Cooking Time: 28 min.

CONTAINER EQUIVALENTS (per serving): ⬤ 1

	Nonstick cooking spray
1 (15-oz.) can	**chickpeas (garbanzo beans), drained, rinsed**
¼ cup	**organic grass-fed butter, melted (or extra-virgin organic coconut oil)**
2	**large eggs**
½ cup	**pure maple syrup (or raw honey)**
2 tsp.	**pure vanilla extract**
⅓ cup	**organic unsweetened cocoa powder**
½ tsp.	**baking powder, gluten-free**
1 pinch	**sea salt (or Himalayan salt)**
¼ cup	**semi-sweet (or dark) chocolate chips**

1. Preheat oven to 350° F.
2. Line 9 x 9-inch baking pan with parchment paper. Lightly coat with spray. Set aside.
3. Place chickpeas, butter, eggs, maple syrup, extract, cocoa powder, baking powder, and salt in blender (or food processor); cover. Blend until smooth.
4. Add chocolate chips; mix by hand until blended.
5. Evenly spread batter into prepared pan.
6. Bake for 25 to 28 minutes, or until a toothpick inserted into the center of brownies comes out clean.
7. Cut into squares.

TIP:

You can also use an 8 x 8-inch pan to bake brownies. They will be a little thicker.

VARIATION:

You can substitute cannellini beans for garbanzo beans. They make a little smoother brownie.

NUTRITIONAL INFORMATION (per serving): Calories: 106
Total Fat: 5 g   Saturated Fat: 3 g   Cholesterol: 31 mg   Sodium: 95 mg   Carbohydrates: 13 g   Fiber: 1 g   Sugars: 8 g   Protein: 2 g

Recipes containing the GF icon are designed to be gluten-free, but please read product labels for each ingredient to ensure this to be the case.

PEANUTTY PEANUT BUTTER SQUARES

SERVES: 16 (1 square each)   Prep Time: 20 min.   Cooking Time: 23 min.

CONTAINER EQUIVALENTS (per serving): 1   ⬤— 2½

	Nonstick cooking spray
1½ cups	all-natural smooth peanut butter
½ cup	raw honey (or pure maple syrup)
2 tsp.	pure vanilla extract
2	large eggs, at room temperature
½ tsp.	baking soda, gluten-free

1. Preheat oven to 350° F.

2. Lightly coat 8 x 8-inch baking pan with spray. Set aside.

3. Combine peanut butter, honey, extract, eggs, and baking soda in a large bowl; mix well.

4. Evenly spread batter into prepared pan. Smooth top with a spatula.

5. Bake for 20 to 23 minutes. Squares may be a little soft when coming out of the oven, but they will continue to cook.

6. Cool. Cut into squares.

NUTRITIONAL INFORMATION (per serving): Calories: 182
Total Fat: 13 g   Saturated Fat: 3 g   Cholesterol: 23 mg   Sodium: 158 mg   Carbohydrates: 13 g   Fiber: 1 g   Sugars: 10 g   Protein: 7 g

Recipes containing the GF icon are designed to be gluten-free, but please read product labels for each ingredient to ensure this to be the case.

RASPBERRY-FILLED COOKIE BITES

SERVES: 12 (1 cookie bite each)   Prep Time: 1 hr.   Cooking Time: 40 min.

CONTAINER EQUIVALENTS (per serving): ½

1 cup	**fresh or frozen raspberries**
¾ cup + 2 Tbsp.	**water,** *divided use*
¼ cup	**raw honey**
2	**large egg whites (¼ cup)**
2 Tbsp.	**fresh lemon juice**
½ tsp.	**pure vanilla extract**
2 drops	**natural red food coloring (optional)**
½ cup	**sifted almond flour**

TIPS:

- Don't limit yourself to raspberries. Any fruit jam (made using the directions above) will make a great filling!

- If you have a stand mixer, this would be a good way to beat the egg whites. If you don't, you might have someone slowly pour the honey mixture while you beat the egg whites.

- Natural food coloring can be found at natural food stores or online.

1. To make raspberry filling, combine raspberries and ¾ cup water in a small saucepan; cook, over medium-high heat, stirring occasionally, for 10 to 12 minutes, or until berries have broken down and liquid becomes slightly thicker. Refrigerate to cool.

2. To make meringue, place honey and *remaining 2 Tbsp.* water in small saucepan; cook, over medium-high heat, stirring occasionally, until mixture reaches 240° F. with a candy thermometer.

3. While honey cooks, place egg whites and lemon juice in a clean, large metal mixing bowl; beat until soft peaks are formed. Set aside.

4. When the honey mixture reaches 240° F., transfer it into a clean, heat-resistant pouring vessel (like a Pyrex measuring cup).

5. Slowly add honey mixture (in a thin stream) to egg whites, whisking vigorously until completely mixed.

6. Add extract and food coloring (if desired); continue whisking vigorously until the meringue forms stiff, glossy peaks.

7. Gently fold in almond flour; mix until well blended. Set aside.

8. Preheat oven to 300° F.

9. Line two baking sheets with parchment paper. Set aside.

10. Transfer meringue mixture into a large resealable plastic bag (or pastry bag). Squeeze out any excess air and seal bag. Cut off about ½ inch of the bottom corner of the bag.

11. On each prepared baking sheet, pipe out 24 1-inch rounds, evenly spaced. Firmly tap each baking sheet against the kitchen counter a few times to release any air bubbles.

12. Bake for 18 to 20 minutes, or until macaroons have risen about ⅛ inch. Remove from oven. Cool before removing from parchment paper.

13. Spread 1 Tbsp. raspberry filling on the flat side of each of twelve cookies. Top each cookie with the flat side of a second cookie to make a sandwich.

NUTRITIONAL INFORMATION (per serving): Calories: 53
Total Fat: 2 g   Saturated Fat: 0 g   Cholesterol: 0 mg   Sodium: 10 mg   Carbohydrates: 8 g   Fiber: 1 g   Sugars: 6 g   Protein: 2 g

Recipes containing the **GF** icon are designed to be gluten-free, but please read product labels for each ingredient to ensure this to be the case.

SCIADONE (ITALIAN EASTER PIE)

SERVES: 12 (1 slice each) Prep Time: 30 min. Cooking Time: 1 hr.

CONTAINER EQUIVALENTS (per serving): ⬜ 3 ⬛ 1 🥄 1

Easter pie was a family tradition for the Calabreses—and this is a unique one because it's a little more savory and a little less sweet. It required a little tweaking to make it healthy enough for this book, but it means so much to me and is such an important part of my family tradition that I wanted you to experience it too.

1½ cups	**all-purpose gluten-free flour**
½ cup	**almond flour,** sifted
½ cup	**coconut flour,** sifted
¾ tsp.	**sea salt (or Himalayan salt),** *divided use*
⅔ cup	**olive oil,** frozen
4	**large eggs,** *divided use*
½ cup + 2 Tbsp.	**raw honey (or pure maple syrup),** *divided use*
1 lb.	**part-skim ricotta cheese**
¼ cup	**agave syrup (or raw honey or pure maple syrup)**
½ tsp.	**pure vanilla extract**
2 tsp.	**finely grated orange peel**
½ tsp.	**unflavored gelatin**
1 Tbsp.	**cornstarch, gluten-free (preferably GMO-free) (or arrowroot flour)**

1. Preheat oven to 350° F.

2. Combine gluten-free flour, almond flour, coconut flour, *½ tsp.* salt, oil, *2* beaten eggs, and *2 Tbsp.* honey in a medium bowl; knead gently until all ingredients are well blended and form a dough ball.

3. Press dough into a 9-inch pie pan, evenly covering the bottom and going 1 to 1½ inches up the side. Set aside.

4. Combine *remaining 2* eggs, *remaining ½ cup* honey, cheese, agave, extract, and orange peel in a large bowl; mix well.

5. Sprinkle gelatin and cornstarch over honey mixture; mix well.

6. Pour filling into prepared pie pan.

7. Bake on the center rack for 50 to 60 minutes, or until filling has set.

8. Cool and serve.

RECIPE NOTE:

At three yellow containers, this dessert pie might blow through your allotment in one delicious slice. If you're eating from a lower calorie chart but still want to indulge a little, you can always just eat half of a serving.

NUTRITIONAL INFORMATION (per serving): Calories: 393
Total Fat: 20 g Saturated Fat: 5 g Cholesterol: 74 mg Sodium: 225 mg Carbohydrates: 48 g Fiber: 5 g Sugars: 30 g Protein: 10 g

Recipes containing the **GF** icon are designed to be gluten-free, but please read product labels for each ingredient to ensure this to be the case.

STRAWBERRY-BANANA ICE CREAM

SERVES: 2 (⅓ cup each)   Prep Time: 10 min.   Cooking Time: None

CONTAINER EQUIVALENTS (per serving): ▇ 2

2	**medium ripe bananas, cut into pieces**
1 cup	**frozen strawberries**
1 to 2 Tbsp.	**unsweetened almond milk (optional)**

1. Place banana in plastic bag; freeze for 4 hours, or until completely frozen.
2. Place banana and strawberries in blender (or food processor); cover. Blend until smooth. Add 1 to 2 Tbsp. almond milk, if needed, for creamier texture.
3. Serve immediately.

NUTRITIONAL INFORMATION (per serving): Calories: 131
Total Fat: 0 g   Saturated Fat: 0 g   Cholesterol: 0 mg   Sodium: 3 mg   Carbohydrates: 34 g   Fiber: 5 g   Sugars: 18 g   Protein: 2 g

Recipes containing the GF icon are designed to be gluten-free, but please read product labels for each ingredient to ensure this to be the case.

VANILLA CAKE WITH CHOCOLATE FROSTING

SERVES: 12 (1 slice each)   Prep Time: 20 min.   Cooking Time: 30 min.

CONTAINER EQUIVALENTS (per serving):   2   ■ 1   ●—1

	Nonstick cooking spray
1 cup	almond flour
½ cup	coconut flour
2 tsp.	baking powder, gluten-free
¼ tsp.	sea salt (or Himalayan salt)
¾ cup	unsalted organic grass-fed butter, *divided use*
1 cup	raw honey (or maple syrup), *divided use*
4	large eggs
¼ cup + 3 Tbsp.	unsweetened almond milk, *divided use*
1 tsp.	pure vanilla extract
⅔ cup	organic unsweetened cocoa powder, sifted

1. Preheat oven to 350° F.
2. Coat a 9-inch round baking pan with spray. Set aside.
3. Combine almond flour, coconut flour, baking powder, and salt in a medium bowl; mix well. Set aside.
4. Cream together *½ cup* butter and *¾ cup* honey in a medium mixing bowl; beat on medium speed for 1 minute.
5. Add eggs one at a time; beat until blended.
6. Add *¼ cup* almond milk and extract; beat until blended.
7. Add almond flour mixture to butter mixture; beat until creamy.
8. Pour batter into prepared pan.
9. Bake for 25 to 30 minutes, or until a toothpick inserted into the center comes out clean. Cool on a baking rack.
10. To make frosting, whip *remaining ¼ cup* butter in a medium bowl; beat on medium speed for 1 to 2 minutes, or until creamy.
11. Add *remaining 3 Tbsp.* almond milk to butter; beat until well blended.
12. Add cocoa powder; beat until well blended, scraping bowl occasionally.
13. Slowly add *remaining ¼ cup* honey while beating on medium speed. Set aside.
14. Once cake is cool, evenly spread with frosting; cut into twelve slices.

TIPS:

- You can make your own almond flour by processing 1 cup slivered almonds in a food processor (or blender with a strong motor). Make sure that you blend in 20-second intervals to prevent the almonds from turning into almond butter. 1 cup of slivered almonds yields approximately 1 cup of almond flour.

- If you can't find almond flour in your store, you can look at club stores or online.

NUTRITIONAL INFORMATION (per serving): Calories: 308
Total Fat: 19 g   Saturated Fat: 9 g   Cholesterol: 92 mg   Sodium: 188 mg   Carbohydrates: 30 g   Fiber: 4 g   Sugars: 22 g   Protein: 6 g

Recipes containing the **GF** icon are designed to be gluten-free, but please read product labels for each ingredient to ensure this to be the case.

SHAKEOLOGY

BANANA PEANUT BUTTER BLISS

SERVES: 1   Prep Time: 10 min.   Cooking Time: None
CONTAINER EQUIVALENTS (per serving): ▢ 1 ▢ 1 ▬ 2

½ cup	**unsweetened almond milk**
½ cup	**water**
1 scoop	**Chocolate Vegan Shakeology**
½	**medium frozen banana, cut into chunks**
2 tsp.	**all-natural peanut butter**
1 cup	**ice**

1. Place almond milk, water, Shakeology, banana, peanut butter, and ice in blender; cover. Blend until smooth.

NUTRITIONAL INFORMATION (per serving): Calories: 305
Total Fat: 11 g   Saturated Fat: 2 g   Cholesterol: 0 mg   Sodium: 399 mg   Carbohydrates: 35 g   Fiber: 8 g   Sugars: 16 g   Protein: 20 g

STRAWBERRY-WATERMELON SURPRISE

SERVES: 1   Prep Time: 10 min.   Cooking Time: None
CONTAINER EQUIVALENTS (per serving): ▢ ½ ▢ 1

½ cup	**water**
½ cup	**chopped watermelon**
1 scoop	**Strawberry (or Tropical Strawberry Vegan) Shakeology**
2 Tbsp.	**chopped fresh mint**
1 cup	**ice**

1. Place water, watermelon, Shakeology, mint, and ice in blender; cover. Blend until smooth.

NUTRITIONAL INFORMATION (per serving): Calories: 155
Total Fat: 1 g   Saturated Fat: 0 g   Cholesterol: 5 mg   Sodium: 131 mg   Carbohydrates: 21 g   Fiber: 4 g   Sugars: 12 g   Protein: 17 g

TROPICAL BLISS

SERVES: 1   Prep Time: 10 min.   Cooking Time: None
CONTAINER EQUIVALENTS (per serving): ■ 1   ■ 1

½ cup	unsweetened almond milk (or coconut milk beverage from a carton)
½ cup	water
1 scoop	Chocolate (or Chocolate Vegan) Shakeology
1 cup	frozen pineapple chunks
1 cup	ice

1. Place almond milk, water, Shakeology, pineapple, and ice in blender; cover. Blend until smooth.

NUTRITIONAL INFORMATION (per serving): Calories: 263
Total Fat: 4 g   Saturated Fat: 1 g   Cholesterol: 0 mg   Sodium: 251 mg   Carbohydrates: 40 g   Fiber: 9 g   Sugars: 22 g   Protein: 18 g

BLUEBERRY BASIL DELIGHT

SERVES: 1   Prep Time: 10 min.   Cooking Time: None
CONTAINER EQUIVALENTS (per serving): ■ ½   ■ 1

½ cup	unsweetened almond milk
½ cup	water
1 scoop	Vanilla Shakeology
½ cup	fresh or frozen blueberries
4	fresh basil leaves, chopped
1 cup	ice

1. Place almond milk, water, Shakeology, blueberries, basil, and ice in blender; cover. Blend until smooth.

NUTRITIONAL INFORMATION (per serving): Calories: 192
Total Fat: 4 g   Saturated Fat: 0 g   Cholesterol: 5 mg   Sodium: 300 mg   Carbohydrates: 26 g   Fiber: 5 g   Sugars: 14 g   Protein: 17 g

SKINNY
COCKTAILS

SKINNY CHAMPAGNE BERRY COCKTAIL

SERVES: 1 Prep Time: 10 min. Cooking Time: None

CONTAINER EQUIVALENTS (per serving): ◻ 1

¼ cup	unsweetened blueberry juice
2 Tbsp.	fresh lime juice
¼ cup	champagne
1 cup	ice
	Fresh or frozen blueberries (for garnish; optional)

1. Place blueberry juice, lime juice, champagne, and ice in a large serving glass. Stir to mix.

2. Garnish drink with a couple of blueberries (if desired).

TIPS:

- For a beautiful drink presentation, layer the blueberry juice, lime juice, and champagne. Do not stir before serving.

- If you can't find a good blueberry juice, you can substitute unsweetened cranberry, cherry, or raspberry juice.

NUTRITIONAL INFORMATION (per serving): Calories: 111
Total Fat: 0 g Saturated Fat: 0 g Cholesterol: 0 mg Sodium: 9 mg Carbohydrates: 10 g Fiber: 0 g Sugars: 15 g Protein: 0 g

---

SKINNY MARGARITA

SERVES: 1 Prep Time: 10 min. Cooking Time: None

CONTAINER EQUIVALENTS (per serving): ◻ 1

2 to 3	fresh lime wedges
2 to 3	fresh orange wedges
2 Tbsp.	fresh lime juice
½ tsp.	raw honey
1 cup	ice
1 oz.	100% agave tequila
1 splash	sweet and sour mixer
	Lime slice (for garnish; optional)

1. Place lime wedges, orange wedges, lime juice, and honey in the bottom of a serving glass; muddle until well mixed.

2. Top with ice, tequila, and mixer. Stir to mix.

3. Garnish with a lime slice, if desired.

NUTRITIONAL INFORMATION (per serving): Calories: 104
Total Fat: 0 g Saturated Fat: 0 g Cholesterol: 0 mg Sodium: 7 mg Carbohydrates: 11 g Fiber: 1 g Sugars: 5 g Protein: 0 g

SKINNY PIÑA COLADA

SERVES: 1 Prep Time: 10 min. Cooking Time: None

CONTAINER EQUIVALENTS (per serving): ▢ 1

¼ cup	**coconut water**
½ cup	**cubed fresh pineapple**
1 oz.	**coconut-flavored rum**
1 cup	**crushed ice**
	Fresh pineapple wedge (for garnish; optional)

1. Place coconut water, pineapple, rum, and ice in blender; cover. Blend until smooth.
2. Pour into serving glass; garnish with pineapple wedge (if desired).

TIP:

Use a coconut-flavored rum, pineapple-flavored rum, or a spiced rum to make this refreshing piña colada!

NUTRITIONAL INFORMATION (per serving): Calories: 114
Total Fat: 0 g Saturated Fat: 0 g Cholesterol: 0 mg Sodium: 30 mg Carbohydrates: 13 g Fiber: 1 g Sugars: 10 g Protein: 0 g

SKINNY COCONUT BERRY REFRESHER

SERVES: 1 Prep Time: 10 min. Cooking Time: None

CONTAINER EQUIVALENTS (per serving): ▢ 1

1 cup	**coconut water**
1 oz.	**berry-flavored vodka (your favorite berry flavor)**
1 cup	**ice**
	Fresh mint leaves (for garnish; optional)

1. Place coconut water, vodka, and ice in a serving glass; stir to mix.
2. Garnish drink with mint leaves (if desired).

TIP:

You could also infuse your own vodka with fresh ripe berries. Use 2 cups chopped fruit to 2 to 3 cups vodka. Let sit for 3 to 5 days. Strain and enjoy!

NUTRITIONAL INFORMATION (per serving): Calories: 99
Total Fat: 0 g Saturated Fat: 0 g Cholesterol: 0 mg Sodium: 97 mg Carbohydrates: 7 g Fiber: 0 g Sugars: 7 g Protein: 0 g

AUTUMN'S FAVORITE SKINNY CUCUMBER COCKTAIL

SERVES: 1   Prep Time: 10 min.   Cooking Time: None
CONTAINER EQUIVALENTS (per serving): ▢ 1

6	**cucumber slices (reserve 1 slice for garnish; optional)**
2 Tbsp.	**fresh mint leaves**
1 oz.	**vodka (preferably Grey Goose)**
1 cup	**ice**
1 cup	**sparkling water**
2 tsp.	**St. Germain Liqueur**

1. Place 5 cucumber slices, mint, and vodka in the bottom of a large serving glass; muddle until well mixed.
2. Top with ice and sparkling water; stir to mix.
3. Add a splash of St. Germain; garnish with a cucumber slice (if desired).

RECIPE NOTE:

St. Germain Liqueur is made from elderberry flowers and has bright and fragrant floral notes.

NUTRITIONAL INFORMATION (per serving): Calories: 109
Total Fat: 0 g Saturated Fat: 0 g Cholesterol: 0 mg Sodium: 17 mg Carbohydrates: 6 g Fiber: 1 g Sugars: 4 g Protein: 1 g

SKINNY COSMO

SERVES: 1   Prep Time: 10 min.   Cooking Time: None
CONTAINER EQUIVALENTS (per serving): ▢ 1

1	**fresh lime wedge**
1	**fresh orange wedge**
1 Tbsp.	**unsweetened cranberry juice**
1 tsp.	**raw honey**
1 cup	**ice**
1 oz.	**cranberry-flavored vodka**
½ cup	**sparkling water**
	Lime slice (for garnish; optional)

1. Place lime wedge, orange wedge, cranberry juice, and honey in the bottom of a large serving glass; muddle until well mixed.
2. Top with ice, vodka, and sparkling water. Stir to mix.
3. Garnish with a lime slice (if desired).

NUTRITIONAL INFORMATION (per serving): Calories: 98
Total Fat: 0 g Saturated Fat: 0 g Cholesterol: 0 mg Sodium: 10 mg Carbohydrates: 9 g Fiber: 0 g Sugars: 8 g Protein: 0 g

INDEX

DIETARY INDEX

GLUTEN-FREE RECIPES GF

PALEO-FRIENDLY RECIPES PF

ABOUT THE AUTHOR

Autumn Calabrese is a celebrity fitness trainer, busy mom, and national-level bikini competitor. Creator of 21 Day Fix®— the best-selling Beachbody® fitness program of 2014— and its high-intensity follow-up 21 Day Fix EXTREME®. She has held personal training certifications from the National Academy of Sports Medicine (NASM) and the American Fitness Professionals & Associates (AFPA). Autumn has appeared on the cover of *Oxygen* magazine and her workouts have been featured in *Fitness* magazine, *Shape* magazine, and Active.com, as well as on TV shows like *Home & Family* and *Good Day LA.*